The Brownists in Norwich and
Norfolk about 1580

T0382056

The Brownists in Norwich and Norfolk about 1580

Some New Facts, together with

"A treatise of the Church and the Kingdome of Christ" by R. H. [Robert Harrison?], now printed for the first time from the manuscript in Dr. Williams's Library, London

BY

ALBERT PEEL, M.A., Litt.D., B.Litt.

Editor of *The Seconde Parte of a Register*

CAMBRIDGE

AT THE UNIVERSITY PRESS

1920

TO MY FATHER

CAMBRIDGE
UNIVERSITY PRESS

University Printing House, Cambridge CB2 8BS, United Kingdom

Cambridge University Press is part of the University of Cambridge.

It furthers the University's mission by disseminating knowledge in the pursuit of
education, learning and research at the highest international levels of excellence.

www.cambridge.org
Information on this title: www.cambridge.org/9781316633236

© Cambridge University Press 1920

First published 1920
First paperback edition 2016

A catalogue record for this publication is available from the British Library

ISBN 978-1-316-63323-6 Paperback

PREFACE

IN sending forth this little book, I should like to express the conviction that much information concerning Browne and Harrison still lies buried in the ecclesiastical records of the city of Norwich. I hope ere long to have leisure to unearth sufficient data for a fuller life of Robert Harrison than has hitherto been possible.

I have to thank the Misses Colman; Mr G. A. Stephen, City Librarian; Mr L. G. Bolingbroke, of the Diocesan Registry; Mr F. R. Beecheno; as well as several of the clergy of the city, for facilitating my investigations. To the Dr Williams's Trustees, who gave me permission to print the documents in *The Seconde Parte of a Register* (of which the present document is one), I have already expressed my indebtedness.

ALBERT PEEL.

GREAT HARWOOD,
February 16th, 1920.

CONTENTS

INTRODUCTION

In the present writer's *Calendar of The Seconde Parte of a Register*, II. 64–6, a long document, with the title "A treatise of the Church and the Kingdome of Christ," is briefly summarised. It consists of more than 24 large folio pages[1] (441–465), and is subscribed "Not yours excepte you repent. R.H."

In a note the intention of printing the manuscript in full was declared, and reasons suggested for believing that R.H. was Robert Harrison. That intention is now carried out, and at the same time some new facts brought out concerning a very obscure episode in the emergence of the Separatist movement and in the lifetime of Robert Browne, its leader.

ROBERT HARRISON AT AYLSHAM. 1573–1574

Robert Browne and Robert Harrison were both students at Corpus Christi, Cambridge, the former apparently graduating B.A. in 1572, the latter M.A. in the same year. At the beginning of his *True and Short Declaration, both of the Gathering and Joyning Together of Certaine Persons: and of the Lamentable Breach and Division which Fell Amongst them*[2], Browne testifies to their acquaintance:

"Some of these which had lived and studied in Cambridge, were there knowne and counted forward in religion, and others, also both there and in the contrie were more carefull & zelous, then their froward enimies could suffer.

They in Cambridge were scattered from thense, some to one trade of life, & some to another: as Robert Browne, Robert Harrison, William Harrison, Philip Browne[3], Robert Barker. Some of these

---

[1] More than 21 pp. (533–554) of the "Transcript" volume. For a description of these documents see the Calendar, referred to throughout as Peel, *Cal. Sec. Parte of a Register*.

[2] 1583 or 1584. The work is referred to throughout as "*T. and S. D.*," and the references are to the 1888 reprint. This quotation is on A 1 recto.

[3] William and Philip were probably brothers to the two first-named.

applied themselves to teach schollers ; to the which labour, R. Broune also gave himselfe for the space of three years."

Robert Harrison seems to have adopted the same profession, for it is as an applicant for a schoolmastership that he first appears in the neighbourhood of Norwich. At Aylsham, some twelve miles to the north, was a 'Free School' that was intimately connected with the county city, and, through it, with institutions that Harrison had known in the past, and was to know in the future. Founded by the Mayor of Norwich in 1517, it had as one of its endowments £10 yearly, paid by the Treasurer of the Great Hospital in Norwich, of which the Mayor etc. were Governors. Archbishop Parker, always solicitous for his native county, founded two scholarships in Corpus Christi, and appropriated them to this school, and to a similar school at Wymondham (commonly called Windham). Of the Aylsham scholars, one had to be born in the town, and the other, having been educated at the school, was to be nominated by the Mayor and Court of Norwich[1].

Parker's concern for the school also appears in the interest he took in the appointment of a headmaster in 1573. Of three candidates for the post, Robert Harrison was superior to either of the others in scholastic attainments, and his application was supported by the Mayor and certain Aldermen of Norwich. From letters that passed between the Archbishop, the Bishop of Norwich, and the Mayor, it seems that at his marriage at Aylsham a short time previously, Harrison had asked the Vicar to alter the form of service prescribed in the Book of Common Prayer. He was also said to be very young, to be afflicted with a 'frenzy,' and to have an objection to reading profane authors to children. For all these reasons the ecclesiastical authorities were disposed to look elsewhere for a master, but the civil authorities persisted, and on his promising to live quietly and maintain no faction, and to have no evil or strange opinions, nor to defend such obstinately in the " prophesyings," Harrison was appointed[2].

Less than a month afterwards, however, appearing as god-

---

[1] For these particulars see Blomefield, *History of Norfolk*, VI. 282 and III. 310 ff. Cf. also Parker's will [Strype, *Parker* (1821 ed.), III. 333 ff.].

[2] Strype, *Parker*, II. 335 ff., and Cooper, *Athenae Cantabrigienses*, II. 177 f.

father " to the child of one Allen[1] of Aylsham," he requested the officiating deacon to omit the sign of the cross and make other changes in the Baptismal Order. In Jan. 1573/4, he was therefore discharged from the school.

It is extremely unfortunate that the parish registers at Aylsham only go back to 1653, as the entries at Harrison's marriage and at the baptism of Allen's child would have furnished valuable information.

BROWNE AND HARRISON COME TO NORWICH

What became of Harrison after his dismissal at Aylsham is not clear. Browne, it is known[2], spent three years teaching, and then he too was discharged. After a period at his father's home, he went to stay with Richard Greenham[3], incumbent of Dry Drayton, near Cambridge, a man of saintly life and strong Puritan views. There he meditated on the state of the Church and on matters of Church government, and decided to preach without the licence and authorising of the Bishops, and against all such authorising. For six months he proclaimed this and kindred messages in public and in private, but he refused to receive a stipend or to take a charge. He then fell sick, and, while sick, was forbidden to preach by the Council.

On recovering health, having already[4] "judged that the kingdom off God was not to be begun by whole parishes, but rather off the worthiest, were they never so fewe," he[5]

"sought where to find the righteous which glorified God, with whome he might live and rejoise together, that thei putt awaie abominations. While he thus was careful, & be sought the Lord to shewe him more comfort of his kingdome and church than he sawe in Cambrige, he remembred some in Norfolke whome he harde saie were verie forward, therefore he examined the matter, and thought it his duetie to take his voiage to them ;...So while he thought on these thinges,

---

[1] For the significance of this name, see below, pp. 8–10.

[2] *T. and S. D.*, A 1 recto.

[3] For Greenham see *Dict. Nat. Biog.*, Cooper's *Athenae Cant.* II. 143 f., and *A parte of a register*, 86 ff. Also his *Works*, published in 1599.

[4] *T. and S. D.*, A 3 verso.

[5] *Ibid.*, A 4 recto and A 4 verso. The work was wretchedly printed, a fact which no doubt accounts for the weird punctuation, which is reproduced in the quotations in the text.

& was purposed to trie also in Norfolk the forwardnes of the people,
it fell out that R.H.[1], one whom he partlie was acquainted with
before, he came to Cambridge.   What was his purpose in coming, &
howe he thought to have entred the ministerie, and did use some
meanes to that end, it is needles to rehearse, onelie this I shewe,
that he seemed to be verie careful in that matter, and though he
leaned to much upon men for that matter, as upon M. Greenham
M. Robardes[2] and others, & was careful amisse for the bishops
authorising, yet his mind & purpose might be judged to be good,
and no otherwise but well did R.B. judge of him.”

The chronology of Browne’s life is uncertain, but it is safe to
say that it was probably early in 1580[3] when he was urging
Harrison not to proceed with his plan of seeking ordination from
the Bishops. The result was that[4]

“ R.H. ether chaunging his mind, or disappointed of his purpose,
returned to Norwich wither also, a short time after R.B. tooke his
journie. He came to R.H.’s house whoe then was Maister in the
Hospitall at Norwich. He there finding roume enough, and R.H.
willinge enough that he should abide with him, agreed for his board,
and kept in his house.”

BROWNE AND HARRISON AT “ THE HOSPITALL ”

“ *The* Hospitall at Norwich ” can only mean the Great
Hospital, also called the St Giles’s or Old Men’s Hospital[5].
Founded in 1249, this institution still exists, sheltering at the
present day 200 old people, men and women. In 1547 it was
surrendered to the king, and, with its possessions, was transferred
by the Crown to the Mayor, Sheriffs and Commonalty of Norwich
for the relief of poor people. With the transference, according
to the *Victoria County History of Norfolk,* “ the office of Master
came to an end.” Whether this was so or not is uncertain, but
probably the office was not filled for some time. The present
Master, who is endeavouring to compile a list of his predecessors,
states that “there is no record from 1550–1643, except that from

---

[1] Robert Harrison.

[2] Thomas Roberts, Archdeacon of Norwich, for whom see Index to
Strype’s *Works,* and also below, pp. 5 f.

[3] Cf. Burrage, *The True Story of Robert Browne,* 5–9, and Powicke,
Robert Browne, 19–22.

[4] *T. and S. D.,* A 4 verso. Italics the present writer’s.

[5] Blomefield, IV. 376.

a tablet in St. Andrew's Church it would appear that Will Jackson was at one time Master, and died in 1626."

So far a considerable search has failed to reveal any documentary evidence of Harrison's appointment or tenure of office, but the writer is not without hope that information of value will yet come to light. It certainly seems likely that the Mayor and Aldermen of Norwich, who were Governors of the Hospital, may have appointed as its Master the man they so strongly supported at Aylsham. This may have occurred any time between 1574 and 1580. The phrase "returned to Norwich," italicised in the quotation from Browne immediately above, plainly suggests that Harrison was domiciled in Norwich when he paid his visit to Cambridge. Naturally, living together, Browne and Harrison talked[1] "much and often...about matters of the church and kingdom of God, and of the Lordship and government of Christ."

This at once led to discussion of the attitude to be adopted with regard to the "forward preachers" in the city. A vigorous Puritan movement in Norwich was headed at this time by John More, the learned minister of St Andrew's, Thomas Roberts, Archdeacon of Norwich, and several others.

On Sept. 25th, 1576, these two, with Richard Crick, George Leeds, Richard Dowe, and William Hart, had petitioned[2] some Privy Councillor against "this conformitie of ceremonies." They complained that "there be alreadie 19 or 20 godlie Exercises of preching and Catechizing putt downe in this Cittie by the displaceing of those preachers," and while they protest their loyalty to the Queen, they say:

"wee suffer ourselves rather to be displaced then to yeld to certen things. Our Bodyes, goods, lands, life, Wife and Children be in her Maties hands, onlie our souls, which must be either saved or dampned, we reserve to our God, who alone is able to save or dampne."

Two years later[3], these ministers, except Hart, but with Vincent Goodwin and John Mapes, sent in a form of submission, in which they expressed willingness to subscribe the doctrinal articles, and declared that ministers ought not to refuse to preach,

---

[1] At length, in *T. and S. D.*, A 4 verso—B 1 recto.
[2] Peel, *Cal. Sec. Parte of a Register*, I. 143–6.
[3] *Ibid.*, I. 146.

nor parishioners refuse to attend worship because of the ceremonies.

On this, they seem to have been "restored to preachinge[1]."
A True and Short Declaration makes plain the fact that
Harrison only reluctantly relinquished the belief that progress
toward reformation could best be obtained by supporting these
preachers. In Browne's words[2]:

"Then fell out these questions between them : Whether those
preachers that submitt themselves unto such popish power, or anie
way so justifie, or tolerate it as laweful in some part, or partlie to be
liked & used, can themselves be liked of, or do their duetie as laweful
pastors and preachers ?
Hereat R.H. did stick because of M. Robardes, M. More,
M. Deering[3] & others whome he then did greatlie like off. But
more he doubted, & as it were, drewe back, when he should geve
over such preachers, or else forsake & shrincke from our owne good
purpose. For he would have the consent of such preachers in the
matters that were determined, & also would have them to joine,
though it was made plaine unto him that they nether would nether
could joine, taking that course which they did...."

"THE SUPPLICATION OF NORWICH MEN TO THE
QUEENES MATIE" [1580]

What Browne omits to mention is that at first on his arrival
in Norwich he himself signed a supplication which requested
much the same things as "the preachers" desired, and certainly
did not go as far as the position he had apparently reached ere
he left Cambridge. Possibly the explanation is that the Supplication was already prepared when Browne arrived in Norwich,
and he saw no objection to adding his name. This petition is
printed almost in full in the present writer's *Cal. Sec. Parte of
a Register*[4], which follows the manuscript in giving the date as
1583. An analysis of the document and the signatures attached
immediately produced the conviction that the date (it must be
remembered that the manuscript is a copy, and not the original
petition) was several years too late. Reference to three of the

[1] Peel, *Cal. Sec. Parte of a Register*, I. 146–7.
[2] *T. and S. D.*, B 1 recto.
[3] Edward Deering, for whom see *Dict. Nat. Biog.* etc.
[4] I. 157–60.

175 names[1] is sufficient to prove this—Robert Browne, Robt. Harrison, Hugh Brewer.

Now not only is there no evidence for thinking that Browne and Harrison returned to Norwich from the Low Countries in 1583, but by that time they had reached a stage in their progress toward separation far in advance of the Supplication's position. They no longer desired merely the "planting that holie Eldership, the verie senew of Christs Church," and the "removing the dumbe ministrie, that horrible evill, which filleth hell paunch with the soules of the people"; they had now set forth in print[2] their belief that true churches were to be formed only by Christians gathering out of, and separating from, the world, appointing their own ministers and officers, and this theory they were endeavouring to practise. Internal evidence thus inclined the writer to replace 1583 by 1580 as the true date. Welcome confirmation was forthcoming, in some measure, from documents now in the Muniment Room at the Castle, Norwich[3]. In an assessment for 70 " Calyvers " for the city of Norwich made in 1578, there appears the name of Hugh Brewer[4], one of the 175 " Norwich

---

[1] The writer begs to acknowledge a serious omission in the *Cal. Sec. Parte of a Register.* Reviews of that work almost without exception mentioned the lengthy and exhaustive indexes. They were very lengthy (the Index of Persons occupies 25 pages with names in double columns), but unfortunately, they were not quite exhaustive. A note at the head of Index IV reads: "All the names...are indexed with the exception of the signatories on the following pages: I. 78, 124, 159 f., 275 : II. 189f., 191f., 220f."

I. 159f. contains the signatories to the Norwich supplication, including Browne and Harrison. The Editor would like to confess that if the work were to be indexed again, the 800 signatories previously omitted would be added.

[2] At Middleburgh, in 1582, Browne published three works:

(1) *A Booke which Sheweth....* (2) *A Treatise of Reformation without tarying for anie....* (3) *A Treatise upon the 23 of Matthewe.*

The plural is used in the text because at this time the cleavage between Browne and Harrison had not begun; indeed the expense of printing the books seems to have been borne by Harrison (see below, p. 17).

[3] Case 13, Shelf A, Bundle 1.

[4] Brewer seems to have been a leading Puritan laymen, especially if he is to be identified with "one Bruer" mentioned in an informing letter,

men " who signed the Supplication. In the Muster Roll[1] for the parish of St Andrew's in 1580, Hugh Brewer's name is missing, but that of " Widow Brewer" appears. It seems likely, therefore, that Hugh Brewer had died meanwhile, and that Widow Brewer was his relict. If this is so, the Supplication must be dated before the Muster Roll of 1580, and the conclusion drawn from internal evidence is thus confirmed.

SIGNIFICANT NAMES IN THE SUPPLICATION

Before leaving the Supplication several very significant names attached thereto should be noted.

(1) *Robart Barker,* whose name appears in *A True and Short Declaration,* first[2] as one of the "forward" students in Cambridge, and, then[3] as one that forsook the Norwich company when trials began.

(2) *John Flower.* The name Flower will not be overlooked by those who remember that on New Year's Eve 1588 (Jan. 10th 1589) Browne addressed to " Unckle Flower " a letter[4] which was discovered by Mr Champlin Burrage, and printed by him in 1904, with the title *A New Years Guift.* Can the unknown uncle be John ?

(3) *John Allens.* Here a suggestive recurrence of names must be noted.

(*a*) 1574. Harrison was godfather to the child of one *Allen* of Aylsham (above p. 3).

(*b*) [1580.] Browne, Harrison, and John *Allens* sign a supplication of Norwich men.

dated Dec. 2nd, 1576, from Sir Francis Wyndham to Nathaniel Bacon. [*Stiffkey Papers* (Royal Hist. Soc. 1915), 185 f.] It describes how when Mr More had been "sequestred from his exercyse," and a Mr Holland appointed to take his place, the superseder was called "Turnecote" and accused of false doctrine "by one Cornewall, a mynistr, & one Morley, a baker, & one Bruer" [Leonard Morley is also a signatory of the Supplication].

   [1] This Muster Roll contains the names of nine of the 175 suppliants.
   [2] A 1 recto.   [3] C 2 recto.
   [4] This letter was referred to by Bancroft in his famous sermon at Paul's Cross a few weeks later.

(c) Before 1584, Browne was married to Alice, the daughter "of *Allen* of Yorkshire[1]."

(d) Harrison, who was married at Aylsham in 1573 (name of wife unknown), had, apparently, a brother William, and "certaine sisters[2]," one of whom is referred to as "Sister *Allens*," in Browne's account of the strife in the church at Middleburgh.

The salient passages are (italics the present writer's):

"There were sundrie meetings procured against R.B. by R.H. and his Partkers for certaine tales and slanders wer brought to R.H., which he straight way receeaved, and delt against R.B. the accusations in the first miettinge were, that R.B. *condemned his Sister Allens as a reprobate.* alsoe he saied she had not repented of her abominations in England...[3]."

Any doubt as to whose sister is meant is removed on the following page[4]:

"The faults They Laied Against him [Browne] Were, For rebukeinge *Rob. H. Sister* of Want of Love, And off abhorring the Pastar : Which They Counted A Slander. Likewise for rebukinge her of Judgeing Wrong Fullie on The Printer, Which Was also made a slaunder."

That is to say, "Rob. H. Sister," and "his Sister Allens" are one and the same person, and therefore—dismissing as unlikely the possibility that Harrison had a sister with the Christian name Allens—one of Harrison's sisters married an Allens, or else Harrison himself married an Allens ("Sister Allens" then being a sister-in-law).

It has already been suggested[5] that Robert Browne's wife

---

[1] Blore, *History and Antiquities of Rutlandshire*, is the source of this oft-quoted statement, for which he gives no authority. The Christian name Alice comes from the Achurch register.

[2] *T. and S. D.*, B 1 verso :

"This R.H. confirmed saiing that he found it true; because bie his meanes certaine sisters of his when he taught and exhorted them, were called and wonne."

[3] *Ibid.*, C 3 recto and verso.   [4] *Ibid.*, C 4 recto.

[5] By Dr F. J. Powicke, in his *Robert Browne*, 39 n. It is strange that, having *A True and Short Declaration* before him, Mr Burrage could suggest (*True Story of Robert Browne*, 28) that "Sister Allens" might be Browne's wife, and even stranger that, in his *Early English Dissenters*, I. 108 (pub-

may have been connected with the Aylsham family named
Allen, concerning the baptism of whose child Harrison was
dismissed from his school in 1574, and, as Browne's first child
was born in Feb. 1583/4, it does seem probable that Browne
met his wife during the time he spent in Norwich and the
country round about. The further possibility that Browne and
Harrison married into the same family should not be overlooked;
for although pastors' wives have often been the subject of discussion in Separatist churches—ancient[1] and modern—yet
family relationship between Browne's wife and part of his flock
would add significance to the statement[2]:

"Likewise for his wife there was much a doe, and for the power
and authoritie which the husband hath over the Wife."

A Congregational Church Formed

Whatever the reason that led Robert Browne to affix his
name to the "Supplication of Norwich men," it is evident that
within a short time he had convinced, not only himself, but also
Robert Harrison, that "the preachers" must be forsaken, and
those who were called should form a church of Christian
believers.

The determination of "the companie" is expressed in the
document now printed (below, pp. 35–6):

"therfore ye wise men tarie and spie out your fit time to build the
Lordes house, for it is not yet time with you, & we foolish rash children will, God willing, step to it nowe according to the good hand of
God upon us & will stay no longer for you, as we hath hetherto
done, the Lord forgive us."

lished in 1912, after the publication of Dr Powicke's work), he should give
the name of Robert Harrison's sister as one of the Middleburgh congregation without suggesting that she was the same person as "his Sister
Allens."

[1] The classical instance is, of course, Francis Johnson's congregation
at Amsterdam, the troubles of which are graphically described in George
Johnson's *A discourse of some troubles...* (1603). It is interesting to note
that near the beginning of this volume (p. 7) the writer refers to the "pride
of Mr Brownes wife and the other weomen in the banished English Church
at Middleburgh" as being "a great cause of disagreement betweene
Mr Harrison and Mr Brown," and a possible cause of Harrison's death.

[2] *T. and S. D.,* C 4 verso.

Browne describes[1] the procedure and its results very clearly:

"This doctrine before, being shewed to the companie & openlie preached among them manie did agree thereto, and though much trouble and persecution did followe yet some did cleave fast to the trueth, but some fell awaie, fro [for] *when triall by pursuites, losses and imprisonment came & further increased* then Robert Barker Nicholas Woedowes Tatsel Bond and some others forsooke us also & held back and were afraid at the first. There was a day appointed, and an order taken for redresse off the former abuses and for cleaving to the Lord in greater obedience. So a covenant was made, & ther mutual consent was geven to hould together....Further thei agreed off those which should teach them and watch for the salvation of their soules whom thei allowed and did chose as able & meet for that charge. For thei had sufficient triall and testimonie thereoff by that which thei hard and sawe by them and had receaved of others. So thei praied for their watchfulness and diligence & promised their obedience. Likewise an order was agreed on for their meetings together....But last of all was this thing determined: whether God did call them to leave their contrie and to depart out of England. Some had decreed it to be gone into Scotland....But R. B. being then held as prisoner at London[2] did send downe his answer bie writing to the contrarie. [Reasons given, as also concerning a proposal to go to 'Gersey or Garnsey'].... *But at last, when divers of them were againe imprisoned, thei all agreed and were fullie persuaded that the Lord did call them out of England.*"

R. H.'s "TREATISE"

It is to this period of persecution and imprisonment, roughly 1581, that the document now printed for the first time evidently belongs. Compare with the passages italicised in the above extract these sentences from R. H.'s "Treatise."

T. W. is said (p. 35) to have defended the cause "twise by sufferinge imprisonment in lothsome prison houses, & with Iron fetters." Again (pp. 55–6),

[1] *T. and S. D.*, C 2 recto—C 3 recto. Italics the present writer's.

[2] Apparently this fixes the date as 1581, for in April of that year Bishop Freeke of Norwich wrote to Burghley (Lansdowne MS. 33. 13) saying that Browne has been apprehended near Bury St Edmunds at the instance of "many godly preachers" for teaching corrupt doctrine, his audience having met "in privat howses and conventicles," sometimes to the number of 100. Browne was sent to London, but released after a short time. He immediately resumed his meetings in the Norwich diocese (Freeke to Burghley Aug. 2nd 1581. Lansdowne MS. 33. 20) and was soon in prison again.

"our mynister preched first & we heard him in a Church of lime
& stone, from thence we were driven into the Church yard, from
thence into a house adjoyning upon the Church yard, from whence
we being had to prison after that some of us had got some libertie
out, we got into that Church againe, from thence we were had to
prison againe."

Indeed, so close are the parallels that, although the manuscript
has neither the name of the author, nor the mention of the city
in which the events it describes took place, there can be little
doubt of either authorship or venue. Every clue that can be
followed up leads to Harrison and Norwich, and not a single
one in an opposite direction, and the whole episode fits in
exactly with Browne's *True and Short Declaration.*

A somewhat more detailed examination of the different
points will not be superfluous.

1. THE AUTHOR

The treatise has, both at the head and the foot, the initials
R. H. The slight hesitation which prevents the attribution to
Harrison without a mark of interrogation is due to the fact that
in Norwich in 1576 there was another R. H., whose views were
emphatically Puritan. On May 13th, 1576 this R. H. appeared
before the Bishop of Norwich, and later in the year he addressed
a very outspoken letter[1] to the Bishop, denouncing his tyran-
nical dealing, calling his office unlawful, and boldly defending
"the discipline" and the silenced ministers in the city.

Apparently, judging from another item[2] in the same volume,
this R. H. was named Harvey (Harvie), and to Robert Harvey,
who graduated B.A. at Clare Hall, Cambridge in 1570/1, the
letter has generally been attributed[3]. Nothing more is known

[1] Printed in *A parte of a register,* 365–70, and called in the Contents
List (which, mistakenly, has "R. T.") "A pythie letter." What seems to be
the original letter is in the Library of the Inner Temple (Petyt MSS. 538,
No. 47, ff. 51, 2) ; a manuscript copy is in Dr Williams's Library (Old Loose
Papers, ff. 59, 60).

[2] "The troubles of M. Richard Gawton of late Preacher at Norwich,
about Anno 1576. 20 August." (In *A parte of a register,* 393–400; the
references to Harvey are on pp. 399, 400.)

[3] Cooper, *Athen. Cant.,* attributes it to both Harvey (II. 2) and Harrison
(II. 178). This helps to discount the fact that the same work says Harvey
wrote the document now printed, a statement no doubt taken from

concerning him, but the knowledge of his existence, and the nature of his "pythie letter," alike insist that there should be just a shadow of a doubt when Robert Harrison is called the writer of "A treatise of the Church and the Kingdome of Christ."

Turning to the more positive aspect, some of the arguments in favour of Harrison's authorship have already been suggested.

1. The towns Windham (Wymondham) and Aylessam (Aylsham), both closely connected with Norwich, and in one of which Harrison had lived, are mentioned in the treatise.

2. The document is very similar in tone and content (both in the personal and impersonal parts) to the earliest known writings of Browne and Harrison. No reader of *A Little Treatise uppon the firste verse of* 122 *Psalm* will find it hard to believe that Harrison wrote also the treatise now printed.

3. In his Epistle "To all our Christian Brethren in Englande" prefixed to *A Little Treatise,* Harrison not only states that he had begun a work on Church government, but also relates experiences exactly similar to those described in the present document. It is quite possible that the tractate which fills the first six pages of "A treatise of the Church" was the work to which he refers.

He says (italics the present writer's)

"Concerninge the whiche cause, I did not thinke it laweful for mee (though I coulde have escaped in tyme ynough) to withdraw my selfe into any other place, for myne owne liberties sake, untill I had more openly witnessed the same cause. which when it seemed good unto God, that I with some others should doo, *by abyding imprisonment a certayne time: Then having offered our selves to suffer whatsoever our vexers should lay upon us, and espyinge nothing like to be done unto us, but to bee holden with lingering imprisonement, and that without libertie of communicating unto others the instruction of the same cause, which we professed:* we thought good rather to undergoe some exile (as it were) for redeeming at least some libertie of worshipping God with safetie of conscience. which when we did, and divers of our Brethren, which were willing to come unto us were restrayned: and we were persuaded, that to returne unto them thither, whereas by imprisonment we should againe be holden from them, would little avayle: I have judged that we have bene debters to them to bestow upon them some thing which might helpe to increase their spirituall courage and comfort. In which

Brook, *Lives of the Puritans,* I. 193, which says, without giving reasons: "Mr Harvey appears to have written 'A Treatise of the Church and Kingdom of Christ.'"

behalfe, when the expectation of me and divers others rested upon some, who in the ende did but slenderlie answere, and satisfie the same: Then I, which for my unworthines and poore gifte, hadde thought never to have set foorth any thinge publikely[1], yet was provoked to indevour my selfe, in some parte...to satisfie that want, which I thought to be great. *And I went about a piece of work touching Church governement. But partlie by sicknes, and partly by weying the cost of the print, and finding it to be above my reache of abilitie: I was hindered, and have let staye that worke, untill the Lorde further inable me.*"

2. VENUE

Norwich is not mentioned by name, but neither is any other city or town, except "Windham" and "Aylessam."

It is to be regretted that there are so few names of persons and places in the document, and especially that the name of the church in which the "companie" met is not given.

This omission is common to all contemporary and later writers, except Chambers[2], who, without stating any authority, says St Peter Hungate. No confirmation of this statement has been discovered, nor do the records of the church (now with St Michael-at-Plea) yield any information.

Other churches that suggest themselves as possible are:

(*a*) St Helen's, the church attached to the hospital of which Harrison was Master.

(*b*) St Andrew's Hall, formerly a Dominican Church, in the choir of which a congregation of Dutch strangers had been permitted to worship from 1565[3].

(*c*) St Andrew's Church[4], of which John More was incumbent until 1591/2. A very full manuscript history of the church[5] contains no mention of the Separatist episode, nor does its writer know of any in the church's records.

[1] This suggests that Harrison's other published work, *Three Formes of Catechismes* (1583) was not written until after the *Little Treatise.*

[2] *General History of the County of Norfolk* 1188.

[3] Blomefield, III. 282, IV. 342; Moens, *The Walloons and the Church at Norwich,* 3. A silver beaker, part of the Communion plate of the Church, presented by "Rychard Browne of Heigham" (who died in 1595), is now in the possession of the Misses Colman, of Carrow House, Norwich.

[4] From 1560, when the rights of patronage were purchased for the parishioners, this church has been so far "congregational" as to elect its minister by popular vote.

[5] Written by Mr F. R. Beecheno, who has not only allowed the present writer to examine the work, but also assisted him in other ways.

Up to the present, personal search on this point has been entirely without result, and so far as ecclesiastical records in Norwich itself are concerned, the "companie" seems to have been "sunk without a trace."

3. OTHER PERSONS MENTIONED

The major portion of the treatise consists of a reply by R. H. to a charge of blasphemy made by "Mr Fentome." Evidently T. W. had first written to "Mr Fentome," who had replied, and then R. H. makes the present contribution.

Is it possible to identify "Mr Fentome" and T. W.?

"*Fentome*" apparently was a Puritan preacher, who had been made a nobleman's chaplain (p. 49); had suffered imprisonment for the ceremonies but "in a faire chamber & on a softe fetherbed" (p. 35); and was in the habit of attending meetings of ministers similar to the "prophesyings" (p. 60).

In *Cal. Sec. Parte of a Reg.* (I. 244) is a list of "Ministers in Northfolk resolved not to subscribe," apparently to Archbishop Whitgift's articles at the end of 1583. Among the 64 names are those of "Jo. Fenton" and of "Mr Fenton," who was "not called." Either of these could be the "Fentome" of the document.

"Mr Fenton" was no doubt Edward, Rector of Booton[1] (about five miles S.W. of Aylsham) from 1564 to 1610.

"Jo. Fenton" is more difficult to identify, unless all the contemporary John Fentons mentioned in the Institution Books and in Blomefield are one and the same, as is quite possible. In 1571 Sir Thomas Gresham presented John Fenton to the Rectory of Swainsthorp (5 miles S. of Norwich), the next entry being 1598. Thomas Blundevil, armiger, presented John Fenton to the Rectory of Newton in 1570 (next entry 1576), Newton apparently being Newton Flotman, which is very near Swainsthorp.

The name also appears for the Rector of two adjacent parishes (now united), Beeston (St Lawrence) and Smallburgh.

---

[1] Blomefield, VI. 356. "In the nave; there lieth the Bodie of Master Edward Fentone, Preacher of the Word in Booton xxxxvj yeares, buried in the year of our Lord 1610." The Institution Book in the Diocesan Registry has 1567 for the date of presentation.

For the former living no date is given, but it must be between 1562 and 1579; for the latter the name occurs in 1596. These parishes are some twelve miles from Norwich.

No trace has been discovered of a nobleman's chaplaincy held by either Edward or John, but there were many noblemen with residences in Norwich whose sympathy with "the preachers" would dispose them to appoint Puritan chaplains[1].

T. W., a protagonist of "the companie," is quite unknown. The initials are familiar as those of Thomas Wilcox, joint-author of the *Admonition to the Parliament* in 1572. He, too, twice suffered imprisonment, and was said to have a bitter pen (see below, p. 64), but the two cannot be one and the same. Wilcox's Puritanism never, so far as is known, became Separatism, and in the later years of his life he gave himself to non-controversial writing. A glimpse at the preface to his translation to De Loque's *Treatise of the Church,* published in the year the Norwich T. W. would be in prison, shows the difference. T. W. of Norwich would not have troubled to explain—lest the translation should "fall into the hands of undiscreete readers, and trouble the happy and quiet state of the Church of England"—that "where the Author seemeth to detract from Archbishops, Metropolitanes, Deanes, and other Ministers in this Church of England, and els where, his meaning is not to condemne those titles allowed and attributed to faithfull Pastors in other reformed churches...but to...impugne the tyrannie and pomp and ambition of popish prelacie."

AFTER EVENTS. *Abroad*

The decision to leave England has already been indicated, and Browne has left on record[2] the sad story of the dissensions at Middleburgh. He informs his readers[3] that Harrison had children who died in Middleburgh, and from S. B.'s *The Rasing of The Foundations of Brownisme*[4], it seems that Harrison had

---

[1] This was a very common practice of noblemen who favoured the Puritans.

[2] *T. and S. D.,* C 3 recto—C 4 verso.   [3] *Ibid.,* C 4 verso.

[4] By Stephen Bredwell, 1588. A 2 verso.

financed the printing of Browne's books. Shortly after Browne and a few of his supporters had left for Scotland (the autumn of 1583), Harrison and the remainder seem to have joined Thomas Cartwright's Presbyterian congregation at Middleburgh, but the union was apparently shortlived, as Harrison objected that men coming from "the churches of England" were received without repentance. Cartwright thought Harrison was "one whom the Lord...hath bestowed good graces upon," and endeavoured to secure a conference with him. To a letter of Harrison's he replied at length, arguing that the churches of England were churches of Christ. This answer came into the hands of Browne, who (early in 1585) printed *An Answere to Master Cartwright His Letter for Joyning with the English Churches: whereunto the true copie of his sayde letter is annexed.*

Why did not *Harrison* reply to Cartwright? Why does he disappear so completely from history? The probability seems to be that he died in 1585. Henry Ainsworth[1] says that he died *at Middleburgh;* Stephen Bredwell[2], writing in 1588, speaks of him as if he were already dead, and George Johnson[3] suggests that the dissensions in the church brought about his end.

AFTER EVENTS. *In Norfolk*

The history of such Separatists as were left behind in Norwich and district is very obscure. Their number, even before the departure of "the companie," cannot have been large[4], and the remnant probably met only in secret. Early in 1584,

---

[1] *Counterpoyson* (1608), 41.

[2] A 2 verso; "...of Master Harrisons, who *in his life time....*"

[3] *A discourse of some troubles* (1603), 7.

[4] Cf. Peel, *Cal. Sec. Parte of a Reg.* I. 189, where the writer of an answer to Whitgift's Articles says:

"for Browne and Harrison who are rashly gone *with verie few* from our Church I speake not."

and again,

"Schisme is departure from the church by open division and making private congregations, with refusal of the commen society of the church, which yet, God be thanked, hath not happened *save in Browne and Harison onely.*"

twenty "ministers of Norfolk," in a petition[1] to the Council, declared:

"we have not mainteined anie division or separation from the same Church in anie respect, but have resisted with all our power such as from time to time have envied the peace therof, viz., both papists and other heretiques, and the late schismatiques of the faction of Browne....It may therefore please your Hon...to take pitie upon us and our poore distressed people, whose daunger is now more then in times past by meanes of that late Schisme of Browne, from which we had much adooe to keepe them, even then when by our ministerie there was reasonable plentie of preching, not onelie in our own parishes, but allso in some neighbour Churches about us, which if thei shall see alltogether wanting and the places supplied with such as can doe litle or nothing, as other places are, we feare the unrulie sort will make that rent in the Church, which we had rather be dead (if God so please) then live to behold."

Five gentlemen of Norfolk, writing[2] at the same time in support of these ministers, say:

"Sundrie of these prechers which be thus proceeded against, have much laboured against the faction of Browne, and therin have done exceeding great good in our Countrie, *so as at this present verie few are noted to be of the same evill opinions.*"

Nevertheless, in spite of all the labours of the preachers, Brownism was not killed, either in Norwich city or in the Norwich diocese. A reference in the *Stiffkey Papers*[3] shews that, in 1591, "Bridget, the wief of Thoms Forde of Babingley cometh not to church and is suspected for Brownism but repaireth to the hearing of sermons," and Mr Burrage[4] has clearly shewn that some kind of Congregational organization was maintained in Norwich itself until 1603, while it is well known that several of the Pilgrim Fathers came from the city and surrounding district.

FEATURES OF THE MANUSCRIPT

The first six pages consist of the "Treatise" proper, an exposition of the Separatist position based on the Scriptures, with which R. H. shews himself to be well acquainted. Even here he insists that kings and magistrates should wait for what God

---

[1] Peel, *Cal. Sec. Parte of a Reg.* I. 224.   [2] *Ibid.*, I. 225.

[3] *Op. cit.*, 176. Babingley is near Lynn.

[4] *Early English Dissenters*, I. 187–90.

says to them by priests and prophets, and not *vice versa*, and the preachers are wrong to wait for the magistrate ere they begin to plant churches, build the Lord's house, establish government, and separate the clean from the unclean. The preachers, however, neither build themselves, nor suffer those that would; they allow Antichristian officers to suspend them, and even cry for the magistrate's sword to be used against those that would go forward in religion; all this when they should be renouncing altogether the evil calling of patrons and Lord Bishops, and ceasing the "tithe gathering of good & bad."

In the reply to "Fentome" (18 pages) R. H. shews himself to be an able controversialist with a quick wit and a ready pen. Little surprise need be felt at the vigour of his onslaught on the Puritans[1], who, in the Separatists' eyes, were afraid to demand that which they believed to be right. When the preachers invoked the civil power against those who were striving for objects they themselves had, in part at any rate, declared to be worthy, the Separatists were not slow to charge them with inconsistency and cowardice as well as tyranny and oppression. Altogether the "Treatise" has much in common with Browne's *Treatise of reformation without tarying for anie and of the wickednesse of those Preachers which will not reforme till the Magistrate commaunde or compell them*, as the title of the latter is sufficient to indicate.

R. H. contrasts the close imprisonment that was the lot of "the companie"—"in lothsome prison houses, & with Iron fetters"—with the "faire chamber" and "softe fetherbed" that constituted imprisonment for the preachers. He points out to the Puritans that the Book of Common Prayer they are compelled to use is substantially the Papists' book, as the latter boast continually, and he asks them to renounce their "lettres of

[1] The feeling against the preachers is well illustrated in Browne's words [*A New Years Guift*, 26 and 27]:

"I have found much more wronge done me by the preachers of discipline, then by anie the Byshops...for once imprisonment by the byshops, I have been more then thrise imprisoned by the preachers or their procurage."

disorders," and encourage their people to join the true churches already planted, churches formed not of those forced to come, but of willing people, who "come with as small drawing and as litle noise, as the morning dew falleth upon the grasse." To pray for the coming of the discipline is not sufficient; "lesse of your praiers and more of your help."

To the Puritan lament that few real Christians attend their worship, R. H. retorts that this is "a just plague for all them that make parishes & churches all one." He answers in turn the many charges—some of them contradictory, he says, and others unfounded—made against "the companie" and himself. These include blasphemy, heresy, Anabaptism (no light is thrown on the extent of Brownism's debt to Anabaptism), and schism. Concerning the last, he complains that "we have sought no corners, but were driven from open places into corners, you plucke us out of the house by the haire of the head, & since complaine that we will not tarye within," and further points out that the Puritans twice drove them from the church in which they attempted to worship, and then "Mr F. clappeth his hands & saith what is this but a foule schisme?" R. H. repeatedly turns upon his adversary in this manner; with incisive phrases and homely illustrations he drives home point after point, and so after three centuries his treatise still throbs with life.

He tells Mr F. that "he is an unskillfull cooke that maketh but one sauce for everie meate, & that an unsaverie sauce to[o], which tasteth but onelie in his owne mouth," and that his words are "as a mightie winde, yet our corne will stand unshaken." People attend his ministry, "because when a man can not have candlelight he is faine to leane downe his head to see a glimmering by the coales on the hearth," while sermons in support of Church government without acts are but "faire words that make fooles faine." At one point R. H. gives his opponent "a little aqua vitae to help you to digest this morsell of blasphemie, which hath stucke so long in your stomacke," and his opinion of the preachers is summed up in the illustrations that they are pouring water into a conduit full of holes, and "if your pasture fence lie outwardly broken, you may drive out the swine everie houre of the day, sweating and runnyng your self out of breath, & yet have them there againe so soone as your backs are turned. But cease you to draw water in a bottomlesse bucket, or els the Lord will close up your wages in a bottomlesse bagge."

THE PRINTING OF THE MANUSCRIPT

The manuscript is printed from the MS *Seconde Parte of a Register*, with the following changes:

(1) "u" is changed to "v" for ease in reading.

(2) Occasional contractions are expanded.

(3) In places division into paragraphs has been made.

(4) The marginal references have been put in their proper places.

The pagination of the *Seconde Parte of a Register* is indicated in the margin thus: [451].

A TREATISE OF THE CHURCH AND THE [441] KINGDOME OF CHRIST BY R. H.

QUAESTIO.   Ecclesia Anglicana non est Christi Ecclesia
ARG.   Ecclesia Christi est regnum Christi
            Ecclesia Anglicana non est regnum.
            Ergo non est ecclesia Christi.

CONF. MIN.[1] Ubi Christus non regnat ibi non est regnum eius.
               At in Eccles: Ang: non regnat
               Ergo non est ibi Ecclesia.
CONF. MIN.   Ubi non est vera Disciplina ibi non regnat Christus.
               At in Eccles: Ang: non est
               Ergo ibi non regnat Christus.

The Church of Christ is his Kingdome, therfore where
as this Kingdome of Christ is not, his Church is not.

Where Christ doth rule & raigne there he is King, but
where rule and regiment is taken out of his handes, he is
dispossessed of the right of his inheritance, which is his
Kingdome; but our mynisters[2] confes that we have not the
true Church government, that is as much to say, Christ
his regiment & scepter, therfore thei have not his Kingdome & therfore not his Church.

If thei awnswer that the whole world is the Kingdome
of Christ, & that he ruleth everie where, the question is
not of that ruling wherby he being God equall with the
Father ruleth & governeth all things, but as to him being
man his heavenly Father hath given the inheritance of
Mount Sion, which is his Church, as it is writen: *I have*   Psal. 2[6]
set my King upon Sion, my holy mountaine. Allso: The   Psal. 132
Lord hath chosen Sion and loveth to dwell in it saying, this [13-17]
is my rest for ever, there will I make the horne of David to
bud, for I have ordained a light for myne annointed. This

---

[1] As MS.

[2] I.e. the Puritan ministers, supporters of Thomas Cartwright,
and advocates of "the Discipline."

Sion is the Church, this horne of David is the strength of the scepter of the Kingdome of Christ.

If thei awnswer that in some part thei have this government, because as thei say thei prech the Word which is the scepter of the Kingdome of Christ. First thei are faine to call backe that which thei before have preched, that is, that Church government is wanting. Allso I demaund of them, if there be any patcher or haulter with the Lord, or if thei may yoke an oxe or [*sic*, and] an asse together in the L. tillage. Allso what agreement is betwixt God & Beliall, and what felowship hath the scepter of Christ with Antichrist, that thei should joyne together in government. The Lord is a Jealous God, & will not suffer his honour to be given to another. Lastlie, I awnswer them, that the worde which

1 Cor. 2⁴ is the scepter of the Kingdome of Christ, is his word of message preched with power & authoritie by them which are sent, which prech with governing and governe with preaching. How thei do this shall appeare afterward.

[442] Where the chiefest and highest ecclesiasticall authoritie is in the hands of Antichrist, there is not the Church of Christ, for Christ hath given authoritie to his owne servants, but in the Churches of our mynisters, the L. Bb.[1], Deanes, Chauncelors, Commissaries, & such like, being the popes bastardes, have greater & chiefer authoritie than thei, & exercise authority over them & thei suffer that yoke: therfore thei have[2] the Church of Christ among them.

In the Church of Christ everie man may execute that which our Saviour hath commaunded in the 18 of Matt. concerning the bringing of due complaints to the Church in these wordes: *Tell the Church;* but in the Churches of these mynisters this can not be executed, no not when a wolf is thrust upon the people instead of a shepheard, or any other most grosse & horrible iniquities are done, thei can not complaine to the Church except thei will call the Bbs. the Church, and he [*sic*] is allwaies the workmaster of that mischief of sending wolves & dumbe dogs unto them: therfore thei have not the Church of Christ. Let

---

[1] I.e., Lord Bishops.   [2] "not" omitted.

them awnswer where ever this commaundement of Christ
could be put in practise among them, as in the Church of
Christ may be daylie. Allso Matt. 18 in the Church of
Christ there be the keies of the Kingdome of heaven, to
binde and to lose [i.e. loose] in outward government, but
in the Churches of these mynisters thei have not this
authoritie, but thei must fetch it from otherwhere, namely
from their chappitall Courtes: therfore they have not the
Churche of Christe.

Thei which being put in office by a king, & have given
over their authoritie into the hands of a straunge king, are
traitors to their true kinge, and have not his Kingdome
among them: but these mynisters have betraied the keies
of the Kingdome of heaven, which are committed to them
& the Churches, into the handes of L. Bb.[1] Chauncelors
& Commissaries, which are straunge magistrats: therfore
thei are traitors to Christ, have spoiled his Kingdome: therfore thei have not the Kingdome of Christe or Church.

The Churche of Christe is sanctifyed and made glorious Eph. 5[27]
without spotte or wrinckle: but in their Church thei confes
there are great pollutions: therfore thei have not the Church
of Christe.

We acknowledge there may be manie pollutions in the
maners of men, but being secreat & not openly in-
daungering the state of the Church: but many grosse pollutions openly appearing in the outward state of the Church
government, are such spotts & wrinckles as declare the
Church not to be glorious nor sanctified to Christ: &
therfore to be none of his. *Know yee not that a litle leaven
leaveneth a whole lumpe,* saieth Paule speakinge to have
one evill member cut of[f]. If then one wicked man worthie
excommunication, not being removed, tendeth to the sow-
ring of the whole lumpe, which is the Church, how much
more shall so many wicked officers & so many wicked
men, which use them, & so many wicked guides which

[1] No commas in MS. It is uncertain whether the writer means
Lord Bishops, Chancellors and Commissaries, or Lord Bishops'
Chancellors and Commissaries. The latter is more probable.

submit themselves to them, & so many people, some
ignorant & some willfull which are holden captive by
these guides, & those officers continuinge so long in this
sorte, not onelie make sower, but make to stinke the whole
lumpe of the Church: therfore such Churches be not the
Churches of Christ, seeing thei are all corrupt, and have
done that which is abhominable, there is none that doth

Psal. 14[1]   good, no not one.

[443]
Esay 60[25]
[*sic*, 60[21]]

But this is the commendation of the Church by the
mouth of the prophet: *The people shall be all righteous, the
graft of my planting shall be the worke of my handes, that
I may be glorifyed:* meaning that outward iniquitie must
be far from the children of the Church, and those children
which be planted there be the Lordes plantes: and the
prophet sayeth: *A litle one shall become a thousand, and a
small one a strong nation*: as we may see this day, the whole
bandes of the Lordes enemies can not stand against the
power which the L. hath given to a simple one, speaking
in his name to the confounding of them all.

Esay 60[18]

Allso the prophet speaketh of the Church of Christ:
*Violence shall be no more heard of in the land, neyther
desolation nor destruction in these borders, but thou shalt
call salvation thy walls, and praise thy gates:* but in these
Churches whosoever desireth to live godlie in Christ Jesus,
& to keepe a good conscience, worshipping God without
the bondage of read prayers in popish wise, and beggerly
Ceremonies, thei suffer violence, both of the wicked guides
and of their lordes, and these abhominations of desolation
are set up instead of Christs worship, & of all these
mynisters the moste doe use them, and the rest consent
unto them by holding their peace, increasing the bandes of
them which suffer for witnessing against them, yea thei
cry for the Civill magistrats sword, and still crave more
violence against them, as though thei had not suffered
violence enough at the hands of unlawfull prelacy: therfore
their Church is not the Church of Christe.

The harlot which hath not taken her fornications out
of her sight, & her adulteries from between her brests,

is not the spouse of Christ, noe though shee have bene the mother Church, as it is writen: *Plead with thy mother that she is not my wife:* but to chaunge the true Church offices with false & Antichristian offices, are spirituall fornications and adulteries, which in the Churches of these mynisters, are not yet taken away: therfore they be harlots & not the Church of Christe. Osee 2

In the Church of Christe the horne of David doth budde, & his Crown flourish upon him: but in their Churches the horne of Antichrist doth not onelie budde, but allso flourish, & the Crownes flourish upon the heades of Bs.[1] Chauncelors, Archd: & Commiss: plants which God the Father hath not planted, must be plucked up by the roots before the horne of David can budde & spring: therfore thei have not the Church of Christe. Psal. 132¹¹

In Sion, which is the Lordes Church, *The priests are clothed with salvation,* but in these Churches the mynisters are clothed with destruction, for most of them are blinde guides, and dumbe doggs, destroiers & murtherers of soules, the rest which seem to have knowledge are malitious and obstinate against the Lordes house building, and will not build themselves, nor suffer those that would, so destruction not salvation coming by them, to themselves and other: therfore thei have not Sion, which is the Church of Christ among them. Psal. 132¹⁶

In the Church of Christ thei may easely be discerned from those which are without, as it is writen: *For what have I to do to judge them that are without? do not yee judge those that are within?* but in these parishes all be one felowship, we see not who are within or who are without, or whome we should count for brethren, & publicans by the determination of the Churches censures: therfore these parishes are not the Church of Christe. 1 Cor. 5¹²

The psalme saith thus, *Out of Sion, which is the perfection of bewty, hath the Lord shined,* but thei that speake most favourablie of these Churches confesse that in the outward government the[re] be many imperfections & de- Psal. 50²
[444]

---

[1] See note above, p. 25.

formities which darke the face therof, yea such deformities thei be as make it ouglie as is proved : therfore thei have not Sion which is the Church of God.

Allso of the people of the Church it is writen : *Let the high acts of God be in their mouthes, and a two edged sword in their handes, to execute vengeance upon the heathen, and corrections among the people, such honor have all his saints:* but in their Churches there is not authoritie, nor any such honour to the Saints that thei should execute vengeance and correction upon the wicked, but thei themselves are smitten by the sword of the wicked, & despitefully used for righteousnes sake, yea the guides themselves lay downe their necks willingly and shamelessly to Antichristian officers to be displaced by their suspensions and such like Censurs so farre are thei from binding them in chaines and fetters of iron : therfore thei have not the Church of Christe.

Rom. 12⁴   Paule to the Rom. speaketh thus : *Wheras we have many members in one body, and all the members have not one office, so we being many and one body in Christ, and every one one anothers members: seing then that we have gifts that are divers, according to the grace that is given unto us, whether we have prophecy according to the proportion of faith or an office let us waite on the office or he that teaching on teaching, or he that exhorteth on exhortation, he that distributeth, let him do it with simplicity, he that ruleth with diligence, he that sheweth mercy with chearfullnes:* thus hath the Apostle set downe the offices & callings of the Church & the mynistrie of them: namely of the pastors, doctors, elders, relievers, & widowes, declaring that in the house of God, we are made one anothers members by the diversities of these callings & guifts of grace, wherin we serve one another, but in their Churches thei have not these offices, much lesse the executing of them, neither any guifts of grace tending therto : for if anie such guifts spring up in any, for want of stirring up such guifts & practising it is quenched as the talent hidden in the ground, so that their parishioners are not by these guifts & callings joyned together as felow members, or knit by these as by the sinewes and bandes of the Church: g⁰ [ergo] thei have no[t] the Church etc.

If thei say thei have some of the offices as pastors & doctors, we deny that a parson or vicar placed by a patrone & a L.B. can be a pastor without renouncing that evill calling, & further executing of his dutie, not in tithe gathering of good & bad, but in separating good from the badde, and as for the Doctor, in some few places where he is, he cometh in much after the same maner, joyning with some Idoll shepheard, or some time server, & withdraweth not the people from abhominations mentioned, nor planting the Church among them: so that the light of these Churches is nothing but darknes, & the chiefest order is full of confusion, what then is the disorder of them? these things are not so in the Church of God.

Allso those which persecute the Church of Christe are not the Church of Christe: for Christe is not divided with- [445] in himself, and thei which hate Sion are not of Sion: but thei persecute them which are gathered together in the name of Christe, holding one law & government under him, whome thei are not able to charge with any abhominations unremoved, either in the outward worship of God or in manners: g⁰ [ergo] thei persecute the Church of Christ, & are not his Church.

Wheras thei say we rende ourselves from the Church it is childish: for allthough thei were the Church, we might have one Congregation as many occasions may fall out, so that we joine with another which is the Congregation of Gods people: If thei can prove that we have joined against Christe in anie Antichristian manner, or keeping any Antichristian order, we will returne to them and reforme our selves.

Allso David speaketh thus of Jerusalem: *Jerusalem is* ¹ Psal. 122¹ *builded as a city that is compact together in itself, wherunto the tribes even the tribes of the Lord goe up according to the*

---

¹ For Ps. 122³. In the letter prefixed to *A Little Treatise uppon the firste verse of the* 122 *Psalm*, Harrison says his first intention was "to have spoken somewhat brieflie upon the whole Psalme."

*testimony of Israel to praise the name of the Lord, for there
are thrones erect or set for judgement, even the thrones of the
house of David.* Jerusalem is a figure of the Church, the
thrones of David a figure of the Consistories of Holy Elder-
shyp in the Church, but in their Churches thei have neither
courte nor consistory, Counsell nor Synode holden to our
David, Christ Jesus, nor in his name, but onely those
unlawfull courts, consistories & Synodes holden by the
strength of the Canon law, even the sharpest edge of Antichrists sword, & that by the confession of them all, therfore they have not the Churches of Christe Jesus.

In the 2ᵈ of the Revelat: the mynister of the Church
of Ephesus is commended for labour and patience, not for-
bearing [them] which are evill, examyning them which are
false Apostles, labouring without fainting, yet our Saviour
Christ threatneth him *to remove his candlestick shortly
except he repent, and come to his first love which he hath
left.* Our mynisters deserve bare commendation in any of
these things, as for labour, thei labour well that rule well,
thei are patient that suffer persecution patiently for
righteousnes sake [while] thei have taken a safe way for
not suffering persecution and avoiding daungers: how thei
have forborne the evill even dumbe mynisters, saving in a
wordes [*sic*, worde] of winde, notwithstanding companying
with them, they are witnes which have seene it to their
grief, how thei examine false teachers & mynisters callings,
the Church hath seene more to her hinderance then to her
furtherance: for thei call everie wandering precher that
roveth about, & can spend an hower in a pulpit, howso-
ever it be, & [*sic*, a] precher & a brother: but those
which have a care to walke faithfullie in all the Lords house,
both in their entrance in & folowing their calling, according to the rule of the Word, thei terme despitefullie
by the name of newe Apostles: but I reason thus, besides
all their faults, thei are fallen not onelie from the first love,
zeale, wordes, proceeding there of which were in the Primi-
tive Church: but allso from the state of government which
is a far greater thing, & thei have not repented nor re-

turned being warned, but refuse utterly to returne therin, therfore their candlesticks are removed, though thei ever had had any, therfore thei have not the Churches of Christ, which are the Candlesticks, as Rev. 1²⁰: if thei say thei refuse not, but tary for the advantage of the Civill magi- [446] strats helpe, it is an evill excuse, which will not serve before the Lorde, who will require at their handes those which have perished for want therof.

David speaketh thus: *Be favorable unto Sion for thy* Psal. 50 *good pleasure, build the walls of Jerusalem, then shalt thou* [51¹⁸,¹⁹] *accept the sacrifice of righteousnes, the burnt offering and oblation, then shall they offer calves upon thine aultar:* so that the accepting of our sacrifices, even of all our prayer, & thanksgiving in the worship of God, depend upon Gods favour toward Sion & the building of the walles of Jerusalem. God is favourable only to the place where his honour dwelleth, his honour dwelleth where his Arke resteth, & departeth when his Arke departeth: As Phinees wife speaketh: *The glory is departed from Israel, for the* 1 Sam. 4²² *Arke of God is taken,* but in these Churches thei have not yet brought home the Arke of God from the Philistines, which is Christ bearing his scepter, therfore the glory of God is not among them, & thei refuse to bring it home, & that wilfullie, therfore thei refuse the L. honour. The Arke is the face of God & the presence of his grace, therfore thei not having it in his resting place, nor going about to fetch it in, can not behold the Lord, nor the face of his annointed; then for the walls of the Lordes house thei refuse for to build them, not as the Israelites did in Aggeus 2¹⁵ the daies of Haggai, who prophesied unto them from the Lord, that all which thei did was uncleane, becaus the L. house was not built; for thei being admonished spedelie obeied; neither as the Israelites did in the daies of Nehe- Nehem. 1³ miah & Hanany, which said it was a time of tribulation & reproch because the walles of Jerusalem were not builded, for thei then applied themselves carefully to the worke till it was finished. But as the Israelites did in Psal. 95⁸ Meribah and as in the daies of Massah in the wildernes

Numb. 14^{22} *when they tempted and proved God,* though they had seene his works, and would not enter into his rest, when thei were commaunded, to whom the Lord sware in his wrath that they should not enter into his rest: nowe these which have not the walles of Jerusalem, nor of the temple builded, & refuse obstinately to builde being admonished, their sacrifices are not acceptable, and therfore they have not the Church of Christe.

Exod. 25^{40} The Tabernacle was a figure of the Church, & the L. gave streight Charge that it should be made according to the paterne shewed Moses in the mount: and so our Saviour Christe was 40 daies conversant with his Apostles after his resurrection, teaching them those things which concerned the building of his Church & Kingdome, & the Apost. according as thei received instruction from him so thei builded, & have left us a paterne: now these Churches are not framed according to that paterne, yea thei faile not onely in a pin or hooke or curtaine, which want might be suffered, but thei faile in the chiefe pillars & walls therof; therefore they are not the Churche of Christe.

This being thus manifestly proved, that thei be not the Church of Christe, thei that be gathered together in them are not gathered together in the name of Christe, [447] neither is he among them, neither can thei have the Sacraments which be seales onelie to the promise made to the Church, neither can thei have the worde preched, for *none can preach except he be sent,* & the Lord sendeth none which by open & grosse wickednes endaunger the state of the Church: the open wickednes in them is this, that thei knowing it to be the mynisters dutie & calling to governe the flocke ecclesiasticallie, & seeing the want of this government, stay notwithstanding for further warrant from Civill magistrats, & so by this negligence & slacknes are guiltie of the bloud of them that perish for want of it: allso thei hate to be reformed & are obstinate against them which admonish them of their duty therin: allso thei hate & persecute those which admonish them: allso thei submit themselves to be placed & displaced by those which usurpe Antichristian authority over the flocke, & in their negligence & slacknes mentioned, thei withdraw not the people from open abhominations of Antichrist, no not from blinde guides & dumbe doggs: not planting the Church, nor separating the cleane from the uncleane: but submit themselves to fees, seales, & popish orders, mumbled prayers & many other Ceremonies & popish traditions. Those things thei doe & admit, unworthie the mynisters of the gospell of Christe, wherby thei leade the people astray: so that thei are not sent of Christe, nor come in his name: therfore thei prech not the worde of message, as by authority & power, but onelie speake of the Word of God as a man without calling might doe.

I have bene often moved by divers of my friendes to write to Mr Fentome, for thei have made report to me of a weightie matter, that he hath charged me with, in their hearing, namelie blasphemie: yet I was allwaies unwilling to write because I had small hope of doing him any good, seeing he hath proceeded to such open enmity against us: For we ought to spend all our time, & to use everie occasion & oportunitie, in dealing with those that are most worthie, in whome some good talents of hope appeare, as our Saviour Christe hath commaunded. But seing his stomacke still boiled, & he could not digest that morsell, but powred it out in writing, I have judged it to be most for the glorie of God that I should cleare my self, least any dishonour should be to the L. cause, or any stumbling blocke laied in the way of them, which otherwise would more readilie interteine it.

therfore have I taken in hand to replie upon a lettre, wherin this accusation against me is contained, which is an awnswer to a lettre of one of my felowe brethren: who allthough he hath matched and outmatched his adversarie, & therefore needed not my helpe, yet I have shewed the cause why I tooke it in hand. In which busines I am irke before I begin to deale with such beastly stuffe, as I thinke was not painted on paper by a precher before, yea it were a shame to honour it with a awnswer, if a man were not notably constrained: and thus the lettre beginneth[1]: If thei had bene the open enemies of God, as papists, or any wicked, you would not as you say have complained &c. but because thei are the deare children of God & tenderlie beloved of him, you are as it seemeth therfore bold to insult upon them and so by your rash boldnes have rushed forth without either guide of your minde or stay of your pen. T. W. did verie fitlie allude to that place in the psal.: If it had bene an open enemie which had done me this harme I could have borne it, but it was even my companion etc.: for of open enimyes we never loke for other measure, but a suddaine mischief coming from a companion & a supposed friend goeth to the harte, & causeth an unkinde grief. Now you awnswer (but because thei are the d[e]are children of God & tenderlie beloved of him) these be tender wordes and would better have become your neighbours, to have bene spoken by them of you then by yourselves touching you, but marke the reason. Because he counted them not open enemies, or such as before time had shewed themselves openlie wicked, therfore he must needes count them the deare children of God, as those close & secreat enimies were not evill yea more daungerous then open enimies, which in time when men hope rather to enjoy their helpe & comforte burst forth into open enmitie & hatred, as you & manie of your felowes have done against us: yea you know that the treacherous dealing of Absolom was worse & grieved David tentimes more then the dealings of Shemei: for thus he testified: *behold myne owne sonne which came out of my bowells seeketh my life, how much more may now this sonne of Jeminy, Suffer him to curse &c.*: now if a man should reason thus Shemei was an open enemy to David when he cursed David therfore he was a wicked man: but Abso-

[448]

2 Sam. 16[11]

---

[1] Extracts from "Mr Fentome's" letter are quoted, but it is sometimes difficult to tell exactly where they end.

lom was a secreat enemy when he saide to his father, *I pray thee let me goe to Hebron to render my vow &c.*, therfore he was a good man, he should make as faire a piece of matter of it, as you have done, & this is fine handsell for the beginnyng.

It foloweth (you say it is the Lordes cause not yours)[1], I would to God he had wiser and better defenders of his cause then you, or els I feare it will fall to the ground, & in the fall get a great & deep wound, & so in the end crush you to pouder, except in time ye repent)[1] he saith it is the L. cause and not his, & you denie it not that I see: belike you confesse it franckly, onlie you wish that it might have better & wiser defenders then he is: he hath defended the cause more valiantly then you have done when you were a defender of it: for he hath defended it twise by sufferinge imprisonment in lothsome prison houses, & with Iron fetters, but you defended it once by suffering imprisonment in a faire chamber & on a softe fetherbed[2], & as for wise defenders, it tendeth to the praise of a workman to make his worke handsome with unhandsome tooles: even so the Lord by weake & foolish instruments overturning the wise & strong things of this world, getteth to himself the greater renowne : you know who hath saide, *God hath chosen the foolish thinges of this world to confound the mighty thinges.* Allso, *the Lord hath put strength in the mouthes of babes aud sucklings to still the enemy:* and allso our Saviour Christe worshipped before his heavenly Father & gave thanks that *he had hidden these things from the wise & prudent, and reveiled them to babes:* therfore ye wise men tarie and spie out your fit time to build

1 Corinth. 5²⁷[*sic*,1²⁷] Psal. 8²

Matth.11²⁵

---

[1] Apparently the sentence between the two brackets is T. W.'s, and then the next three to the second closing bracket Fentome's reply.

[2] Cf. *Stiffkey Papers*, 200, where Sir Francis Wyndham speaks of some in Norwich imprisoned for supporting John More of St Andrew's Church : "yt ys to be marveled at how many came to them to pryson, & how they were banqueted, wyne brought to them & on Fryday night even feastes made them in pryson both of fleshe and fyshe."

the Lordes house, for it is not yet time with you, & we foolish rash children will, God willing, step to it nowe according to the good hand of God upon us & will stay no longer for you, as we hath hetherto done, the Lord

[449]
2 Sam. 6²²

forgive us.   Therfore as David awnswered Michol saying *of those maydens which thou hast spoken of shall I bee had in honour.*   See [*sic*, So] say I to you of those verie same foolish defenders which you thinke should be a shame to the L. cause will the L. get glory & renowne to his cause to still & daunt you all.   Then you feare the L. cause will fall to the ground if it have no better defenders: this is wholesome doctrine: it becometh you to know, that whosoever fall the L. cause can not fall, but you, if you

Rom. 3

withstand it shall fall before it.   Paule saieth, *Let God be true and every man a lyar that thou mayest be justified in thy words, and overcome when thou are judged, allso our unrighteousnes commendeth the righteousnes of God:* allso, *the verity of God hathe more abounded through my lye to his glory, and our unbelief can not make the faith of God of none effect.*   If the evill handling of Gods cause by the children of Israel which came out of Egipt could have prevailed against the L. truth (his truth is his cause &

Deut. 1

his cause his truth) then should the rest of Canaan never have bene atteined: but the L. destroyed that generation which sought to turne his truth into a ly, & caried up a new people: so that the L. cause wente forward, but the evill handlers therof fell in their sinnes before the L., whoe made his truth in performing his promise so much the more pretious, when by such notable murmuring he was not hindered, to performe mercy, truth, & covenant on his side.   So if we faile in our defense the L. will make us fall, but his cause shall stand: for he will mainteine his right & cause, he keepeth his throne for that purpose, he will uphold the same for ever.

1 Sam. 5⁴

Now it foloweth that the L. cause in falling should get a great & deepe wound)¹ this is great & deepe divinitie, for Mᵣ F. maketh the L. cause as Idoll, & likeneth it to

¹ The bracket marks the end of the quotation from Fentome.

Dagon the Idol of the Philistines, which in his fall brake
his head & both his handes but Mr F. must marke, that
allthough Dagon gatte such woundes before the Arke, yet
the Arke never gat wound before Dagon, nor yet before
Israel, when thei caried it so untowardly upon the stumbling 2 Sam. 6^{6,7}
oxen, when it should have ben caried upon the priests
shoulders, though Uzzah got a deadly wound, for evill
handling of it.

Now to go forward. T. W. chargeth some of Mr F. side,
that the name of God is much dishonoured & blasphemed
by them. Mr F. awnswereth that speach can not be uttered
by the Spirit of God, & whie? because it is a ly saith he,
& how proveth he that? becaus saith he I for my part
take heaven & earth to record that it is a ly. Now it is
dead sure, as if Mr F. should stand before a judge accused
by some witnesses of some matter of life & death & the
Judges should aske him how he could cleare himself, I will
swere saith he that I am not guilty: but the Judge &
those that stand by will say: I am sory for thee if thou hast
nothing to say for thy self but that. But seing you can no
better clear your self as guiltles, I will a litle help forward
for your inditement, & prove you guilty thus, you cause
the name of God to be dishonoured & evill spoken of,
that is to say blasphemed, by the papists, for thei sticke Matt. 18^{17}
much upon the authoritie of the Church, & cast in your
teeths reprochfully demaunding, where this saying *tell the
Church* can take place, & becaus you can not, as indeed
you are not able to give them any reasonable awnswer in
the point, therfore thei say you have a goodly Church &
a goodly gospell; so the gospell of Christ Jesus is blasphemed
by you, in neglecting to establish the due government of
the Church, that it might appeare where & how such
complaints might be heard, as our Saviour Christ hath
commaunded everie one, by occasion mynistred, to bring
to the Church. I omitte the forme of praiers which you
use, which the papists have boasted full oft in despight of [450]
the protestants, that for all their goodly reformation, thei
are faine to borow their forme of praiers & a number of

Ceremonies of them. It is not time to handle the hundred part of these things, which might be spoken in this cause.

Next of all you aske, where you & your felow deceivers, as it is set downe, have spoken against this government, then you make a great protestation of your praying for it both privately & publiquelie. Lesse of your praiers, & more of your help; the scribes & pharisees praied openlie to be sene of men, & you in times past keeping such a stirre for Church government in the pulpit, & quieting yourselves so quickly when you are out have declared, that you rather would seeme to be the favourers therof, & would lay a burthen upon the backs of others, which you will not lift at with your litle finger but I would see all the sort of you pray as Nehemiah did, who when he had praied, buckled himself to the busines of the wall building, & went closelie to the matter, not making many wordes before he setled to the deed doing.

Then you take God to witnesse that you wish it from the bottome of your hearte. Faire words make fooles faine, but wise men will looke to the deedes. I can tell you where once were spoken as faire words as those, & yet the deedes spake another thing; namely of Saul, when he came from the Amalekites: for he saide to Samuel. *blessed be thou of the Lord, I have fulfilled the commaundement of the Lord* : but Samuel was not so awnswered, but sifted him further & sayde *what meane then the bleating of the sheepe in myne ears, and the lowing of the oxen which I heare.* So I awnswer you, if you wish for this government so intirelye, what meaneth such yelling and roaring, which cause so many pulpits in England to ring against a fewe silly soules, whome you are not able to charge, as swerving anything at all from this government, which you woulde beare us in hande that you love: but sure if you love it absent and farre of[f]: as a man may say he loveth a lyon because he hath heard say, it is a kingly beast, but yet he would be loth to come in the lyons armes: but you neede not to feare this so, except you will be unfaithfull labourers, then indeed you may

Matt. 6⁵

Nehem. 2¹²

1 Sam. 15¹³,¹⁴

feare, for it will kill all such & breake their bones, before thei come at ground. Well, Church government & you then be lovers & friends, but as it should seeme of no great acquaintance, for either you know not her, or she knoweth you : but peradventure she hath chaunged her voice & speaketh like a childe, but the next time she cometh to offer her service, or to checke you for her service refused, she will make a louder rowse in your ears be ye sure.

Afterward you say, you practise it to as far farre[1] as your consciences are assured by the Word you may: & so you leave the practise therof allso, as far as your consciences are perswaded you may: & even so did Saul destroy the Amalekites & their cattell, for he thought in very conscience, that a few of the fairest of the cattell, for no worse end then the Lordes sacrifice were better spared the[n] spoiled : but as Saul was reproved for not doing the whole will of the Lord, so shall you be reproved for not practising the whole Church government, in all points as the L. hath commaunded, the L. will not be awnswered with (as far) that same as farre, squoreth for as[1] evil conscience :

And in that you say your consciences are assured by the Word : this is but a dazeling of your owne eies, & a foule begging of that which is in controversie, of which kinde of Logick, your whole lettre consisteth : we know manifestly there is no word of God, which permitteth a mynister to slacke his duty in any point; yea if the sinne of Saul was so great in sparing some of the Amalekites ; what is the sin of our mynisters in England which spare [451] to separate the prophane from the holie, seing the death of the bodie is so much lesse then the death of the soule : them whome the Lord hath given charge, that thei should be given unto Sathan by separation, will he lesse severelie aske account of their slaughter then he did of the slaughter of the Amalekites.

But our mynisters awnswer that thei separate some, because perhaps once in a few yeers thei keepe backe some

[1] As MS. This paragraph seems to have been carelessly written.

whoremaster that is a poore siely rascall, from the L. table, & which was never of the Church: but the fat cobs, which be whoremasters, userers, oppressors, forestallers, common swearers, undoers of the poore men by the law, ignorant of the most groundes of christian religion, thei will talke with thes afterwarde: even such a reckoning made Saul to[o], for he killed the evill favoured ones, but the faire & fat ones he spared: but the Lord as he was jelous then, so is he now, & if he could not suffer those enemies unslaine, which once many yeers before had shewed one cruell part toward his Church, how will he now suffer unslaine with the scepter of his sonnes Kingdome, those unholie wretches, which still day by day do prophane his sanctuary? he will not do it but cause in his jelousie the lives of them which have spared them for their lives, as was saide to

1 King. 20^{24} [*sic*, ^{42}] Ahab concerning Benhadad by the mouth of the prophet.

Now it foloweth in your lettre, you tell me your judgement is that our prechers crept in at the window/[1] alas your judgement is verie siely and weake judgement, & as it is weake so is it fowlie corrupted, & wo to the Church that should stay on so weake a staffe: there is all you say for that: alas this is yet the simplest awnswer that ever I heard in my life: those prechers whosoever thei be are pitiously beholden to you, who hearing such a great matter against them, & taking upon you their defense, & that with a man of so weake judgement as you say should be able to help nothing at all in such a pinch: peradventure you sought for your arrowes & thei were lost, therfore you came & saide, what should you shoote at such a litle white: but go to I will make it a litle broader that you may see it: you & thei have confessed, that the Lordship & superioritie which the BB. have over the flocke is unlawfull, & not standing with the simplicitie of the gospell; if you be not still of that minde, signify to me against the next time, & I will bestow the labour to prove it: if it standeth not with the gospell of Christe it

---

[1] From this point in the MS. the close of many of the extracts from Fentome's letter is marked with a line, thus: /.

is against Christe, & so Antichristian, but the BB. by
the vertue of the superiority & lordship have given you
your lettres of disorders, & by that calling you come in,
& upon that calling you hold, & by commaundement
from them you & thei will cease your mynisterie, as divers
of the chiefest have spoken & done, & therfore your
entring in was by antichristian meanes, so not being by
Christ which is the doore, it must needes be by the window.
Now if you have any strength your self, pluck down this
window, which is set up in your way:

then after T. W. concluding that we can not heare you,
you awnswer onely to the conclusion, & say, we can not
becaus we will not, & we will not becaus our will is not
ruled by Gods will, how prove you that? but you leave of[f]
& fall to threats saying that both will & power shall be
taken from us, & the doore shut/. Nay we will not becaus
we dare not, & we dare not becaus the Word of the Lord
hath bound us by many streight commandments, as this
for one, *Save yourselves from this froward generation :* ene[1] Acts 2⁴⁰
that froward generation of whome he speaketh there, held
the grounds of religion better then you, as we are able
to prove : & that you are froward it appeareth for that
nothing will perswade you to do that which you acknowledge
to be the mynisters duty, therin we charge you of negligence
& flat disobedience. Paul chargeth Timothy with a
solemne charge : *to keepe all those things inviolate wherof* 1 Tim. 5²¹
he gave commaundement, which chiefly in that Epist. were
about Church government : but you have not kept them,
neither will professe to keepe them : so you uphold this
horrible sinne of disobedience with a high hand, which
endaungereth the state of the Church, most grievouslie,
& you colour all this with a cloake of tarying for further
authority, & yet you say you are sent of God, & called
of the Church, & yet you stay for further authority then
these 2 offered you, for this cause which containeth in it a
great sort of especiall causes yf I had time to speake of
them, you continuing unreformed, & frowardly with- [452]

---

[1] I.e., e'en = even.

standing admonition are seven times worthie to be separate from the Church your selves, that is the cause that we can not joine with you in any felowship, much lesse in the felowship of worshipping God together with you.

then for alledging this saying of our Saviour Christ *My sheepe heare my voice, a straunger will they not heare:* You say it is like our other doings, So it is, & your awnswer is like your other awnswers: you must not cast it out of your handes before you have unknit the knot. I have proved that you are double worthie separation, all such are strangers, & may not eate of the L. passeover, therfore if we should heare you, we shoulde heare the voice of straungers. You say we bow and bend the Scripturs as pleaseth our heades; are you not ashamed to awnswer after this maner? is it enough to awnswer another man that he wresteth a place of Scripture, & not tell him in one word short or long, how he wresteth, & where the fault is? whie have you set downe no places which we have bent & bowed? thei bow & bend the Scripturs to their owne measure, which make the commaundement of government of the Church a litle commaundement, & teach the people that it may be tollerated, to be still forborne, & so thei breake that which thei count a litle commaundement, & teach men so, therfore the Lord hath spoken of such that thei shall be litle in the Kingdome of God. But for wrong alledging of the Scripture, you have used a good caveat in this letter, for you have not cited one place of place[1] of Scripture in this long lasie lettre: but onlie borowed a couple of phrases from thence, as good never a whit as never the better. this is notable barrennes, but the L. will drie you up more, if you take not heede.

It foloweth (your tale of a messenger you might have put up & used at another time & to another people; as for us we have our warrant from the L. who hath sealed our calling surely in our conscience, & the children whome the L. hath given us, are allso our Epist. writen in our harts/. the tale as you call it of the messenger may not

Exod. 12⁴⁵

Matt. 5¹⁹

---

[1] As MS.

be put of[f] until another time, neither can it be fitlier
applied to any people then to you, it sitteth neare your
skirts, it is no marvaile though you would be ridde of it,
but tarie, it will talke to you againe: yf a gentleman send
his man to borow mony at his neede, & he go & borow
a cloake & no mony; is there any hurt in the cloake
borowing may the servant say, yet it is but a cloake
& no mony, & therfore will not serve his masters turne,
so it was but a pranke of an evill messenger: even so you
mynisters are sent on this errand, first to plant Churches,
which is the speciall building of the L. house, excepte you
had come unto them not as ruinous houses, but as Churches
visiblie planted: & then you are to do in the L. house
such things as you are commaunded: if you build not the
house, your other labour is but lost, So Aggee witnessed Agg. 2¹⁵
to the Jewes, that their sacrifices & all that thei did was
uncleane, till the temple was builded: much more then is
your preching uncleane: for the true spirituall house being
unbuilded, which should sanctifie all unto you, & speciallie
when you refuse to do it being charged, which the Israelites
refused not against the charge of the prophet Aggee, &
yet behold a greater then Aggee hath the Lord sent to
speake unto you: for you know he which is leaste in the Matt. 11¹¹
Kingdome of Christ is greater then he: well then you are
set to worke in the vinyard, but becaus of a litle flash of
water which was in your way, you fearing to go over your
shooes, have turned aside into the field, & wrought there
all day: will your master accept of it when you come home,
though you say you have wrought? nay, but he will say
becaus you were not in the vinyard, nothing is done of that
which I would have had done, the messenger whome the
Lord sent to cry against the aultar in Bethel did his whole 1 King. 13²
message, but failed onely in a circumstance, in that he did
eate bread in that place being greatly inticed by another
prophet: but the L. brought upon him the reward of an
evill messenger; & what will he then do to those which
faile in the first & chief point of their message: we say
that the beginning is more then the half of any thing: &

indeede if any of you could shew a Church planted allthough it were but of ten Christians, it were more worth, then the half, yea then the whole that ever you have all done yet:

Now to defend you from strokes which are due unto an evill messenger, you have your stale excuse, that is the warrant of your concience, wherby you say the Lord hath sealed your calling /. how should I know that? you testifie of your self therfore your testimonie is not good: even so I have heard of a man, which being taken with a fault, was threat to be put to death: nay saide he I shall not dy for this: how knowest thou that quoth the accuser? I thinke so quoth he. thus doth Mr F. seale all his warrants unto us, by my conscience is so perswaded, & the L. hath so sealed my conscience: either the Word of God hath given him over, or he hath given it over in this defense: for we have not from thence one proofe of matter neither [one or two words missing].

2 Cor. 13²
[*sic*, 3²]
Mr F. proceedeth & saith: the children whome the L. hath given us are our Epist. writen in our harts: adde therto, which is understood and read of all men, or els you are but a mangler: this is one of the 2 phrases of Scripture which I spake of, & yet it cometh before it is wellcome 2 Cor. 10¹⁸ as we shall see anone. Paule saieth *he which praiseth himself is not alowed but he whome the Lord praiseth;* but no marvaile though you make much of a litle, for you measure your selves with your selves & compare your selves with your selves: but we will compare you a litle with the Apost. whose glorie you have clothed yourselves withall, & plucking of[f] your stollen feathers, we shall see that you are naked, & as far from the glory of the Apost. as you are neere his maner of speach. Paul planted many Churches, so that the worke of his handes appeared, & gave testimony that the grace which God had given him was not in vaine; yea the verie Churches being his building in the Lord were a testimonie of his calling: therfore as manie Churches planted by himself, so manie epistles or lettres of certificate be to be read of all men, that he was sent of God, & that the good hand of God was upon him:

therfore so manie of you as have bene so long in the mynisterie, & can not yet shew a Church planted, do wante your chief testimoniall & epist. which should commend you unto us, as ministers sent of God: therfore instead of ministers you must goe for vagabondes, untill you can shew us this testimoniall: but then we will receive you in the name of the Lord: now we heare your wordes, but then we should see your works, & know your power.

Our Saviour Christe being demaunded whether it was he that should come or thei should looke for another, awnswered not thus: I am he that should come: but saide, *goe shew what thinges you have seene & heard: the blinde receive their sight, the halt go, the leapers are clensed, the deaf heare, the dead are raised up, and the poore receive the ghospell:* so our Saviour Christe did not compell any to receive him further then he made the works which by the testimonie of the prophets pertained to his calling apparent in the sight of all men: Which works the prophet Esay beareth record unto in the 61 ch. thus. *The Spirit of the Lord [is] upon me, therfore hath he annointed me, he hath sent me to preach good tidings to the poore, to binde up the broken harted &c.:* as he speaketh of his works answering therto in the 11 of Math. Therfore allso in the 5 of John he saieth: *I have greater witnes then the witnes of John, for the work which the Father hath given me to finish, the same workes that I doe beare witnes of me that the Father sent me:* but you have no outward witnes at all, but inward, by the witnes of conscience as you perswade yourselves. But we aske you, are ye the true ministers sent of God or shall we looke for other? except ye canne awnswer thus, behold what is seene, we have our Churches planted, the uncleane separate from the cleane, all open abhominations of Antichrist expelled, & our poore flocks redeemed from his iron yoke, & governed by the due order of Christs government, & we have the keies of outward binding & losing, without borowing them from any Antichristian Courte[1]; and so forth manie things more, as the Word of God hath measured

Matt. 11[4,5]

Esay 61[1]

John 5[36]

---

[1] "yoke" crossed out in MS., and "Courte" substituted.

[454] out the lines of your dutie : we must needes awnswer you that it is not you that be sent we must needes seeke up others. But ye will say ye have after a fashion Churches in your parishes, for you would els be ashamed to bragge thus. Looke upon the Church of Corinth which Paul calleth his Epistle, though you amonge you make it a verie deformed Church, as I have heard with myne eares, see if you can

1 Cor. 1⁵ know your owne by it or it by yours. Paul witnesseth thus of them, that thei were *ritch in Christ in all kinde of speach and in all knowledge,* so that thei were not destitute of any guift, wating for the appearing of our Lord Jesus Christe : but now see the children which the Lord hath given you as you say, of how manie can you say, loe here was he borne ? Indeede there were manie in whome some good towardnes did appeare, which resorted to you Mr F. because when a man can not have candlelight he is faine to leane downe his head to see a glimmering by the coales on the hearth. Yet if a man should aske a question, if you were their father, were not the children forwarder then their father. I know manie of their harts were grieved at the patching of your prayers, & some of them have not letted to tell you of it, who indeed were the chief begetters of those children, by fruitfull edifying of gratious speach & godly conference, of whome you chalenge to yourself the honour of parentage. But be it that the Lord gave some blessing to your labour, when you laboured somewhat against Antichrist, you now refusing to strive lawfully and to reforme your self and your charge, according to the L. his commaundement, but bearing your self an open enemie to them which are forwarder then you, be sure the Lord will cut you shorter, & give you a barren wombe and dry brests : & in token therof these children, whome you spake of, the chief of them have forsaken you, & yourself have missed a gratious time, wherin you might have wrought such a worke by them, as would have comended you, both before God & his people, & for your default, the honour is given to another though it grieve you. Thus your Epist. wherof you boast, is writen with the lettres so wide asunder that no bodie can reade it but your selfe.

It foloweth the marke of the beast, which you say we have upon us is utterlie untrue/. this is the truest thing which I had yet: for you may say that & sweare it to[o] that it is a false marke, & witnes of a false calling.

It foloweth we are surely perswaded, that we are of the number of those, that are marked by the marke of God in their foreheades/. Mʳ F. scripture is nothing but surelie perswaded, & perswaded in conscience : he is an unskillfull cooke that maketh but one sauce for everie meate, & that an unsaverie sauce to[o], which tasteth but onelie in his owne mouth : well it is all we can get, we must hold us content till better come.

But note that T. W. objecteth concerning the marke of the mynisterie, the marke of outward profession, & Mʳ F. awnswereth of the L. election. But let that go it is one of the least faults: that you have the marke of the beast we prove, for everie Antichrist is the beast, & of the beast, but you have received their waxen seales in your handes, & their handesfull of benesons on your heades, whome I before proved to be Antichrists, & you do not repent in nor renounce it : therfore you have received the marke of the beast. If not, teach me what the marke of the beast is, I would learne. And that the marke of God in your forheades doth not appeare I prove it thus : thei onelie were marked by the marke which mourned & cryed for all the abhominations that were done in Jerusalem, but you account notable abhominations of Antichrist but pretty tollerable spots and imperfections, therfore your mourning & crying must needes be therafter, as it appeareth without care or jelousie : neither doth the zeale of Gods house eate you up, neither doth it pitie you to see her stones in the dust. Moses spake softlie, but the cry of his praier was exceeding loude : but you declare that in speaking verie loud, you pray verie softlie, so as surelye persuaded as you are if you looke not to this matter, your worke will be worne out before you be aware.

In that you charge us as marked with impudencie, it is but a bare taunt, we will beare more then that against

Ezech. 9⁴

[455]

Exod. 14¹⁵

our selves: but whether we give you any taunts in wordes onelie without matter & notable occasion ministred, and that not in our owne private cause I submit it to the judgement of all men. You say, if we hold on the course we have begun we shall shew our selves impudent to the world. Judge you not to be verie skillfull of the right way your self, which can tell others that thei are out of the right course, & speake not one word when thei went out, no where, nor how thei should come in againe.

It foloweth as for coming in the name of Gods enemie, I have shewed before my certificate in conscience /. You thinke you are of good credite with us, or els you would at one time or other bring some surety out of the Word of God more sufficient then your owne conscience: you will make your conscience weary & overcharge it, if you lay all upon it. but I rase your conscience thus: you came not in the name of Gods friend, therfore in the name of an enemie, for he that is not with him is against him: if you came in the name of Gods frende you would surely doe that you are sent for, & discharge your message at least in the chief points therof: for he tha[t] *loveth God will do his commaundement:* therfore you not planting the Church which is everie ministers dutie, to doe when he seeth it undone, even with as much speed as Nehemiah & those that were with him builded the

Nehem. 4³⁵ wall, which put not of[f] their clothes all the while, but
[*sic*, 23] for washing, till the worke was finished: you declare that you came not in the name of a lover of God, for allso thei that love him love his glory, & the increase therof, & that with jelousie, the increase of Gods glorie is especiallie in enlarging the boundes of his Church. how can that¹ boundes be enlarged, before thei be set, when thei are set, then it appeareth from day to day who are added to the Congregation, as appeareth in the first planted Church by the Apost. & the number of them which increased is set downe in three places at the least in the Acts,

Acts 1¹⁵, 2⁴, according to the time of their increasing: even so you, if
5¹⁴, 6⁷, 4⁴

¹ As MS.

you could have planted the Churches, should have seene what harvest the Lord would have given to your sowing from moneth to moneth, & from day to day: but wheras now you can not tell whether you have more or fewer, at thend of those many yeers then you had at the beginning. You your selves have latelie complained, some of you that you have none, & some of you that you have but one that feareth the Lord, in any outward appearing in your parishes: even a just plague for all them that make parishes and Churches all one: & those few which you have, if thei waxe more forward then your selves thei finde heavie friends of some of you.

You are charged that you seeke flesh & bloud for your arme, you cleare your selves of that, & howe? I see (you say) clearlie with the eies of my soule, that I am free from that curse which thei deserve which make flesh & bloud their arme, & therfore you pray that your adversarie may see it to[o], & you count him dimme sighted because he can not see it, & this is all you can say for your self: if we stand in doubte that the eies of your soule are dimmed in this matter, what shall we be the hender[1], thus you may tell a wise man, & kepe your self unwise still: the Lord make us to get more wisdome by your punishment, then we are able to do by your instruction: for full well I see that that the Lord taketh when it pleaseth him wisdome from the wise, words from the eloquent, & grace from them that have abused it, by sinning to quenching of it: but to come to the matter: They which account them selves mynisters sent of God, & allowed by the Church, staying from their dutie for further strength from the Civill Magistrats, to make them strong in their mynisterie, make flesh & bloud their [456] arme: allso to you, Mr F., thei which get them selves in, to be noble mens Chapplaines, as thinking therby to winn credit to the gospel, & some backing to them in their mynisterie, do extoll the strength of man, & abase the

[1] "hender" repeated in margin. Probably means "nearer." See "Hend, Hende" in *New Eng. Dict.*

strength & glorious scepter of Christ Jesus, & so take
flesh & bloud for their arme: now as cleare as you see
with the eies of your soule that you are cleare from this
evill, more clearlie we do heare with the ears of our bodies
that this evill hath overtaken you.

It foloweth wheras you say, we leave all obedience
till we be commaunded; indeed we are loth to come before
we be commaunded as you do, but rather waite with
patience & praier, what the Lord will say by the mouth
of godlie & Christian Magistrats/. Often have I heard
that Kings and princes should waite what the L. should
say unto them by the mouth of prophets & priests, but
never the contrarie, that the prophets or any mynisters,
should waite what God should say to them by the
mouth of Magistrats, except you meane by their mouth
their sword. This is a browne bred loafe of Mr F. owne
moulding, even so evill moulded, that it breaketh asunder
so soone as one toucheth it, yea it is such a lumpe of
leven, that if it should fall into a whole batche of dough,
it would marre all: & no marvaile though their bread be
very sower which use to leven all with this. but let us
assay to put away their leven, by the sweete Word of
God: Saul taried for Samuel to heare what he should say
to him from the Lord, because he taried not for all the
great haste till Samuel came who taried longer then appointment, therfore the Lord cast them of[f]. David
being himself indued with the spirit of prophecie yet
waited what the Lord should say to him by the mouthes
of prophets and seers: for he saith in one place to Zadock,
art thou not a seer? I will tary in the fields of the wildernes
untill there come some word from you (meaning Ahimaaz
and Jonathan the priests) to be told me: he allso did attend,
what the L. saide unto him by Nathan the prophet &
Gad the Seer. Ezekiah sent to Isaiah for an awnswer
from the L., upon the despightfull dealing of the Assirians.
Josiah searched for a prophet, to aske Counsaile what the
L. should say to him, & finding none in Judah but
onelie a woman prophetesse Huldah waited carfullie what

1 Sam. 13^{13}

2 Sam. 15^{27}

2 Kings 19^2

2 Kings
22$^{13, 14, 15}$

the Lord should say to him by her: but now I heare a
whispering that the priests in Judah waited for Josiahs
reformation. Indeed we have offten hearde such things,
wofull disputers be thei all: those priests waited for reformation, as the wicked people of England waite for
death: for the longer it tarieth the better leave shall it
have: yea so waite allmost all our mynisters & people
to[o] for Church government, for thei know it is a heavy
friend for their licentious living: but say in good sadnes,
did those priests well in taryinge unreformed, till Josiah
constrained them? yea thei did see well, that thei kindled
the consuming fier of Gods wrath, which for all the re- 2Kings22²⁰
formation of Josiah would not be quenched in the land,
but his jelousie sustained him, & his arme was stretched
out still.

Yet behold the best pretence our mynisters for their
waiting, alas a wofull pretence, is this: & have not our
Christian Magistrats commaunded all the mynisters in this
land, to guide their flocks by the rule of the gospell of
Christ Jesus: yf it be so wherfore do thei waite unreformed against their owne knowledge and conscience:
but to proceade. It is written in the 9ᵗʰ of the 1 of Samuel:
In Israel when a man went to seeke an awnswer of God, 1 Sam. 9⁹
thus he spake, Come, let us go to the seer: but Mʳ F. will
teach us a better way though not so readie, the priestes
lippes were wont to keepe knowledge, but now belike the
case is altered, so when a man hath a evill matter in hand
it will shame the Mʳ¹: Well then Mʳ F. hath put his
hand to the plough, and now he standeth & looketh
backe, wherfore thinke you? for one that should come &
bring the whip after him, and therfore when it cometh, [457]
my sentence is, that he should have the first handsell of
it, for if he had not bene more lasie then the horses, then
there had bene ploughed by this time of the day more
then an akre of ground: but a loitering servant he is glad
to have such an excuse to stand still, yea hee quarelleth
with us because we go on saying we be not commaunded:

¹ Master.

4—2

but I would have him awnswer me if this trumpet have
not yet sounded to us to the marching, or his standerd

Psal. 20⁵·⁷

have not yet bene displaied, which hath said, *I am with
you to the end of the world, but we rejoice in the salvation
of our king, and set up our banner in the name of our God,
when the Lord performeth our petitions of dwelling in Sion:*
thei waite for flesh & bloud, but we waite for the name of
the¹ L. our God: they are brought downe and falne, but
we are risen and stand upright, and having turned our
backs upon the Antichristian Egipt, we are prest &
readie to goe with our true Josue even Christ Jesus, unto
the place where the L. hath pighte² his tabernacle: yea
the L. hath saide a great while since *how long will it be
ere this people will go up?* yea all this time of quiet peace,
which the L. hath given us in this land, for which you say
we are not thankfull, hath bene the patience of the Lord
waiting for our going up into his rest, even the visible

Ps. 84⁶
[*sic.*?132¹³]

Church: *for in the middest of Sion his honour dwelleth,
and there is his habitation for ever.* Judge then who are
unthankfull, thei which despise the loving suffering of the
Lord, by not returning from Babilon to him in Sion, or
thei which are obedient to the heavenly voice which
speaketh, thus *Seeke ye my face*, this is our obedience to
go through the vale of wearines digging fountaines to
quench our thirst, till we appeare before the L. in Sion.

But because I have bene long in this former part,
& the more worke we do, the more we have to do, to set
this disordered geare in order, even for redeeming the
time, wherof we have small store which may be better
spent then in going over everie part, I will take but a litle
of the scumme to cast in the fier, & suffer the rest to
vanish away in the smoke till it be consumed. Thus T. W.
confesseth that he can not discerne how this or that thing
should be, therfore (saieth he) must he needes confesse
himself blinde / this is as good a reason: Mʳ F. could
never see a white crow nor a blacke swan, therfore Mʳ F.
is starke blinde. Now afterward goeth to prove *schis-*

¹ "name of the" repeated in MS.   ² I.e. "pitched."

matiques, & how ? first (saith he) because we draw the people from the true preching of the Word of the eternall God. Here is the best side turned out, & that with a goodly glosse set upon it, of true preching of the word of the eternall God : I awnswer you with Job : *Will you speake wickedly for Gods defense, and talke deceitfully for his cause, will ye accept his person, and will ye contend for God ? is it well that he should seeke of you ? Will ye make a lye for him as one lyeth for a man ?* though the wordes of your mouth be as a mightie winde, yet our corne will stand unshaken : for we are free from the things wherof you accuse us, but the evill lighteth upon your owne pat[e]s. how prove you that ever we did draw any from the true preching of the word of God ? yea we call them to it with all our power, and use what meanes we can to have the exercise of the Word preched to flourish among us.

But I see well enough you have forsaken the feare of the Allmightie in that you throw out your railings you care not how sclaunderouslie. But I know your disease : we come [not] to you nor to your felowes, therfore not to the worde preched. I deny your trifling argument : We have the Word preched among us. we have proved that you stand excommunicate, till you be reformed, therfore we refuse your felowship, & you for spight to revenge your [458] quarell, & to make the matter heinous say we refuse the Worde. No I say, not the Word but you, & not you so soone as you have either cleared your selves or re- formed yourselves in those things wherof we charge you. for you standing in these open abhominations, indaunger- ing the state of the Church preching not the worde of message, as we shall see anone. But you say you prech Christe : the Divells confesse Christe, must we go heare them therfore ? but of your preching occasion is given to speake anone.

You charge us allso with drawing the people from the Sacraments : we embrace them dulie mynistred, and the true use of them thei are seales to the promises & the promises are onelie to the apparent Church. for it is

Ps. 128⁵   saied: *the Lord from out of Sion b[l]esse thee, and there*
Ps. 133³   *the Lord appointed the blessing and life for evermore:*
Levit.   but contrary wise it is writen *he that bringeth his sacrifice,*
171⁻⁵   *and not to the doore of the tabernacle of the congregation,*
          shall bee cut of[f] from the Lordes people: so the Sacra-
          ments are not dulie ministred, nor the Worde dulie
          preched, but in the apparent Church, & about the ap-
          parent Church planting. As for publique prayers from
          which you say we draw the people: if you meane read
          & stinted prayers in popish wise, we had rather you
          should be at them then we: We pray publiquely when
          the congregation meeteth, you say prayers when your
          parish meete, grudge not at our praying, & we will not
          envie your saide prayers: but ever you goe on, that we
          draw the people: we would be ashamed to hale & pull
          the people as you do. I thinke you feare that all the
          best will away: we drawe none but whome the Lorde
Ps. 110³   draweth by touching their consciences: yea *the youth of*
          our wombe be the willing people, which come with as small
          drawing and as litle noise, as the morning dew falleth upon
          the grasse.

          Now cometh your heavy quarell against me: namely
          blasphemie, for that I should call preching pratling as
          you say. I deny that ever I called preching pratling, the
          Lord is my just Judge, prove it, it standeth you in hand
          for your honesty: for you have accused me more then ten
          times: but this was saide, when you had nothing to say
          for your selves, but allwayes obtend this worde preching
          preching. I saide that preching without power, or preching
          by them which are not sent, is no preching but rather
          pratling or as the sound of brasse and a tinckling
          Cimball: that it is no preching. I prove it by Paules doc-
Rom. 10¹⁵ trine, for he saith *how can they preach except they be sent?*
          Now I say none such as by open abhominations, as sub-
          mitting themselves to Antichristian Church government,
          or such like sinne do openlie endaunger the state of
          the Church, can be sent of God, or come in his name; for
          thei can not so much as be of the Church so long as thei

continue. Now Mr F. I have given you a litle aqua vitae
to help you to digest this morsell of blasphemie, which
hath stucke so long in your stomacke. Then you recken
up other things wherewith the prechers are charged,
thinking it verie absurd : & to it you go againe twise
before the end of your lettre, as to be blinde guides,
deceivers, & such like; you guide us not up to Canaan
the Lordes rest, but leade us up into Egipt: for you
governe us but not according to Christs true government
which you confesse to be wanting from you : therfore you
are blinde guides : allso you are placed & displaced by
the BB : therfore when we have most neede of you, you
are gone : this is deceiving; if it were nothing but this, for [459]
I speake of one of the last [? least] matters: for so accounted
Job of his friends, saying, *my brethren have deceived me as* Job 6^15
a brooke, and as the rising of the rivers they passe away :
in time they are dryed up with heate and are consumed, and
when it is hotte they faile out of there places, or thei departe
from their way & course, they vanish and perish : now
I say that thei that went from about Windham considered
them, and thei that went from about Aylessam, waited for
them, but thei were confounded when thei hoped, thei
came thither and were ashamed . I could as easilie prove
the rest but for wasting of time : but here is enough
proved untill you disprove it, either by writing or which
I had rather if it were the Lordes will, by shewing your
selves other men.

Then you charge us that we perswade the people to be
rather in houses and in corners then to be where there is
the publique face of the Church : that is as much to say that
the Congregation can not publiquelie meete in a house,
except it be a great house of lime & stone. But M^r F.
& manie mo deale with us thus thei set bandoggs on us
to baite us from their doors, & since thei looke out and
say there came no bodie there, and thei chide us when
thei meete us, because we came not to their house. for
our mynister preched first & we heard him in a Church

---

¹ The meaning is not clear.

of lime & stone, from thence we were driven into the Church yard, from thence into a house adjoyning upon the Church yard, from whence we being had to prison after that some of us had got some libertie out, we got into that Church againe, from thence we were had to prison againe. Yet now we are charged as people which will not come to the Church, thus reasonablie are we dealt with. Now Mr F. clappeth his hands & saith what is this but a foule schisme? It should seeme he is foulie ignorante what a schisme is, that called it a foule schisme to go from a great house for the Church exercises to a lesse : he hath heard somewhat of a schisme & he hampereth about it : but Mr F., a schisme is this to make a wilfull departing from that which is the apparant Church of God. Put on your harnesse againe, & fighte till you prove this by us, & we will cast downe our banner and betake ourselves to your mercie.

Then you say we cover this schisme with errors & heresies: this is scarce either rime or reason, to cover schisme with an heresy. Mr F. covereth one ill favored speach with another: nay if we should cover we would turne the best side outward, & cover foule things not with fouler then thei but with fayrer. a man going to market to sell a bushell of brandie wheat will not lay a litle dracke or darnell on the top of it, for then his market were done: but we are not ashamed of our wheat, neither do we cover it: it is faire & cleare thanks be to God & good seede, wheras yours is full of durcockle & tar[e]s of your owne devises, which I will name anone, & for feare least those Chapmen which looke on our wheate should never buy of yours after you saying to them that our corne is nought before thei see it; but prove any error or heresie, even the least shew therof in us, even the bredth of an heare, we will cleare our selves or reforme our selves: if you can prove none we must call unto the L. the righteous Judge of our innocencie, to coole the heat of such tongues, whose words are as sharp as razors or as the coles of Juniper.

Now concerning your selves because you speake what

you list, you must heare what you list not. I cannot discommend your wisdome in covering, for you cover wiselie
in your kinde, covering many errors & heresies with a
faire pretence of true preching, & you adde the word of
the eternall God, this is to cover, & to paint over the
coveringe, but let us remble or remove, & see what is [460]
underneath. You teach that a true mynister lawfullie called
must stay for authority from the Civill Magistrate, if thei
be Christian for reforming his charge by Ecclesiasticall
government. You teach that he must waite what the L.
saith to him by the mouth of the magistrate, you teach
that a man may receive the Sacraments of blinde guides
and dumbe dogges, and that he ought so to doe, if there be
none other in the parish, you teach that thei be Sacraments
by what man soever thei be mynistred: you Mr F., have
taught that blinde guides and dumbe dogges are, after a sort,
builders of the house of God: you teach that the commaundement of Church government is lesse then other
commaundements; you teach that Church government
(& so Christ's government of the keies of binding &
losing) is not matter of salvation, that is as much to say Matt. 16¹⁹
that which is bound on earth by that meanes is not bounde
in heaven nor contrarywise: you teach that it is a handmaide to doctrine, making the kinglie office of Christ but
handmaide to his office of teaching: you teach that a man
may receive the Sacraments in company of them which are
knowne open offendours: you teach that there can not be
due separation of cleane from unclean without separating
the soule from the bodie: you teach that thei which are
starved for want of spirituall foode by Idoll Shepheards that
can not feede, must with humble suit attend upon the BB.
& patrones curtesie, till thei bestow better upon them:
you teach that a shepheard which can feede, ought notwithstanding to leave his flocke at the commandement of the
Lordly Elders which usurp authority over them, yea though
it be but for a quarell of bringing them into subjection to
a tradition of men as a white linen garment & such like:
you teach that those things which are amisse in your

4—5

Church are but imperfections not hindering the peace of
the Church, & that no man may disturb the peace which
you have for them. Alas what peace so long as the whore-
domes of Jesabel even the whore of Babel do remain? thes
things you teach & an 100 more I dare take upon me to
name, which be grosse errours, & some of them overturning
the groundes of religion, being upholden of you with high
hand, are even plaine heresies.

Eccles 10¹   Thus you digg pitts and fall into them your selves:
dead flyes cause to stincke and putrefy the ointment of the
Apothecary; so doth a little folly him that is in estimation
for wisdome and for glory: so thei being so many dead flies
of errours amongest your ointment of some true doctrine
which you speake make all to stinke, & especially this
great lumpe of dead carion of your frowardnes against the
L. building, being not a litle follie but a great mischief do
make you & your felowes, which heretofore were estemed
for wisdome & loving even contemptible, & even as a
Job 8¹¹   rush which was greene sometime, & fadeth for want of
mire, for your estimation must needes fall if you be not
faithfull in all the Lordes house: for that is the upholding of
your credit, and even your wisdome and honour before all
people.

T. W. did aske you a question or two, & you did bid him
awnswer them himself. *K[n]owledge should dwell in your*
lippes: but you know, if you should have awnswered them,
you should have bene as well shackled as thei which should
have awnswered our Saviour Christe about the baptisme of
John.

2 Thess. 3⁶   Next the place of Paul being cited to separate our selves
from them which walke inordinatly: you say if we meane
as Paul meaneth we must looke to our felow disciples for
Idlenes, as you charge us afterward: Thinke you that the
Word is not more generall, because Paul used it against
those that walke idlie, therefore he meant none other? you
shew your cunning: if you heare a man sweare, & you say
to him he that breaketh Gods commaundements is accursed,
and you say to him you meane to touch him specially for

that present time, therfore do you meane to charge nobodie [461]
els, therfore a whoremaister standing by, whose[1] you knew
not, may say with himself, he meant the swearer: But you
runne on as though you had the winde at the sterne, and
as though T. W. had got a staffe for his owne backe, you
plucke it out of his hande, & fall a beating of him and
us with it: you charge us for not labouring as before, for
letting our wives and children wepe for want, for going
backward with the world & waxing poorer. The Israelits Exod. 5[2]
were counted grievouslie oppressed, because straw was
taken from them, & thei had not made their whole tale
of bricke, yet had thei their handes and legges at will, &
the field before them to scratch up stubble & such poore
fewell as thei could finde: but we are more cruellie used,
for we were shut up betwene walls most of us, with our
leggs chained, all of us put to great expense, & those
which were out of prison not able to stirre out of the doors,
when thei were at home, nor able to be at home except it
were a litle by stealth, for the bursting open of our doors
& violent handling, yet now we are beaten by M[r] F.
tongue & others, because we have made no more bricke,
& coined no more money. You know M[r] F. what was
our let, except we should have done as you did in prison,
to have taken money of them that would have given it us,
for then we could have saved some part of our charges: but
we know we shall have things enough cast in our teeth,
though what you know by any of us we can not tell. I for
my part do not know any of our companie poorer then thei
were at the beginning of our trouble I thancke God hartily
but I know some of the companie richer even in outward
things which is even the mercifull bountie of God, who is
our shepheard. therefore we want not, *he prepareth a table* Psal. 23
for us in spight of our foes, he annointeth our heads with
oyle and our cuppes do overflow, and for his kindnes and
truth we desire to spend our dayes in his house.

Whose wives you should meane to have wept for want
I know not, but if Moses wife called her husband *bloody*

---

[1] ? Either mistakenly for " whome" or else a word is omitted
following it.

husband, because [of] the Circumcision of the childe, we
will not thinke it straunge though some mans wife of our
companie call her husband poore husband because of the
persecution of the Church allthough her husband be no
more in fault, except it were in tarying to[o] long, before
he put his hand to the Lordes busines then Moses was in
faulte for the circumcision of the childe, saving that he
drave it of[f] to[o] long. But Mr F. what if we should loose
houses, landes, or all the rest of our goods, wives, children
and all, (as we durst make none other reckoning, if any
better measure come we shall put it among our gaines)
what then I say, would you checke us by our povertie and
miserie: it is our glorie and not our shame, we have received
all from the Lord, and we hold all in our handes, even with
our lives, to offer to the Lord, at his good pleasure, thinking
it a happie thing, if the Lord will vouchsafe to serve his
glorie, of any thing that we have, and if we maie make us
such a debter of our *unrighteous Mammon,* we are happie,
for that whatsoever we lay out[1] in silver, he will pay it in
gold and pretious stones, and seven times the weight,
heaped measure, pressed downe, and running over.

[462]
Hebr. 10^{25}

You charge us with running from house to house, we
are commaunded by the Apostle to exhort one another and
that so much the more because the day draweth nigh:
now we can not do much except we meete often, and goe
one to anothers house, if we behave not our selves well
when we meete blame us: now I have awnswered for our
idlenes[2], let us come a litle to your sore working: there
are a companie of prechers as thei call them about you,
& you use to go 2 or 3 daies a weeke on foote or on
horsbacke, as the weather maketh most for your ease, half
a dosen miles perhaps, as it falleth out more or lesse, &
there you spend an hower in a pulpit, to get a litle praise,
to commend or discommend one another[3], and all the day
after feast & talke of prophane things; all this may you

---

[1] "out" repeated in MS.

[2] Transcript mistakenly has "weakness."

[3] Norfolk was a stronghold of the "prophesyings," which seem to
have been continued in some districts after the general suppression

do and say with the frier *heu quanta patimur:* but sometimes you feast not but fast, but after a worse maner then
did the Pharisees, whome our Saviour Christe reproved as
fasting to be seene of men: for you fast in open sight, and
cause all the people to do so: and in the meane time there
is nothing named as the cause of the fast, nor any thing
at all reformed: yea the governors of the exercise most
unreformed of all: We reade in the Scripturs of better fasts
then these which the Lord rejected. But some of the
prechers I graunt are more carefull & sober, and worke
some what better then this cometh to, both in sermons
making and studying: but though thei rise earlie thei are
never the nearer, so long as thei poure their water in a
conduite which hath so manie holes, except thei provide to
stop, though thei should toile never so sore, yet should
their worke be never the more seene: & if your pasture
fence lie outwardly broken, you may drive out the swine
everie houre of the day, sweating and runnyng your self
out of breath, & yet have them there againe so soone as
your backs are turned. But cease you to draw water in a
bottomlesse bucket, or els the Lord will close up your
wages in a bottomlesse bagge.

Afterward you charge us to ly one on another using one
anothers liberality, saying you feare that the communitie
of the Anabaptists and family of love will fall among us:
now I must needes liken you to the children to whome our
Saviour likened the froward generation which would not
daunce when their felowes piped unto them, nor weepe when Matt. 11[16]
thei mourned to them. for we help one anothers wants as
we are able, & you say behold Anabaptists and men of
the family of love: some of us as you beare us in hand
weepe for want, & you say behold bankrouts & beggers:
if you had but one drop of that Charity which is not
suspitious you would rather hope of that communitie
which is spoken of Acts 2 & 4 would flourish among us
then misdeeme that the communitie of the Anabaptists
should fall in among us: but we are despised & cast
downe, therfor you passe litle to spurne us: Well you

feare for that which will come after, & you accuse us,
but it is of that which we shall do, or you feare we will
do, indeed such things you prech: there are will witnes to
your face Mr F. that you spake thus in a pulpit, *surely this
matter will prove an heresy:* so you being not able to
charge us with heresy (as we defie you all therin in the
name of the L., do it if you can) you charge that we shall be
heretiques hereafter. Seldome have I read in the hystorie
of the Bible of any which accused other of that thei would
do afterward, except their surmise were grounded on something going before: as in Ezra 4 certain enimies accused
the Jewes, that if the city should be built thei would
withhold their tribute from the king. Indeed they had
plaied so with Nebuchadnezzar, hard before the captivity:
so though thei were spightfull enimies, yet had thei some
pretence for their cruell suspition: but without any reasonable colour of pretence, or liklihood of heresie to charge
us that we will surelie be heretiques I can not finde a yard
wand in all the Scripturs of so large a scise as to measure
this outstretched crueltie, but of the divells shap[e] as
mention is made in the 1 & 2 of Job, for there the devill
beholding Jobs singular innocency yet is bold to say to
God that if he will handle Job thus & thus he *will
blaspheme him to his face,* even thus are we accused that
if we might have libertie we would prove Anabaptists.

Ezra 4
[463]
Jer. 52³

Job 1¹¹, 2⁵

Therefore Mr F. you may see that you being not able
to finde any example of any wicked man, to shape your
cruell surmizings by, have shaped them by the divells owne
paterne. But he tormoiled¹ with cruell mischief &
brought forth a lye, so shall you. And lastlie, for lying on
anothers charge, you may evill checke us by it, for we are
content when we meete, with a drie morsell, and we take
what heede we maie of that inconvenience: but some of
your company have so used the matter, I wot where, that
you have made one kitchin to chaunge her Ma². you make

---

¹ From *tormina*, acute colicy pains.
² The meaning of this is not clear, except that the preachers are
charged with securing refreshment at the Queen's expense.

us bewitched & beside our selves, because we have meate
& will not eat it, we dare not eat that meat which hath
poison in it, neither dare we receive our meat at the carving
of those servaunts, whome our householder hath charged
not to meddle with ordering the house: so it is not for
malice as you charge us but for feare of our Masters dis-
pleasure: & that our Master hath forbidden you to order
his house, till you be reconciled to him, we have proved.

Next after T. W. saying that the L. hath opened his
eares to heare the charmers voice, you say you thinke so,
& yet you say he refuseth to heare the prechers voice:
as though he that stoppeth his ears at the voice of the
true prechers of Gods Word, may not be saide to be like
the deafe adder that stoppeth his ears at the voice of the   Psal. 58⁴
charmer. But if a man take Davides meaning thus, that
one which singeth sweetlie can not with his sweet singinge
charme an adder from his sting: what can you except
against the exposition, which is more probable in my
judgement then the other, all though I leave it free. But
you know common speach speaketh thus such a tongue
would be charmed, which is not meant by enchantment:
allso who hath bewitched you, that is, so greatlie deceived
you, & it is not meant by witchcraft, but by false teaching
as Paul speaketh to the Galath.

But let that go, you in the next line of your letter,
whilest Charmer is fresh upon the tongue, compare us to
sorcerers, because we go into corners, as you say: We have
sought no corners, but were driven from open places into
corners, you plucke us out of the house by the haire of the
head, & since complaine that we will not tarye within:
We love not the darke, you have *loved darknes more then
the light,* as the light it self bewraieth and will bewray, to
all those to whome God have given & will give eies to
see. I pray you Mʳ F., were those of whom the Author to
the Hebr. sayeth *they lived in dennes and holes of the earth,*   Hebr. 11³⁸
were thei sorcerers or like to sorcerers: so you see our
going into corners maketh us no more like sorcerers then
our persecuted forefathers have bene; & your standing

in pulpits maketh you no more like publique teachers then the popish priests have bene. But let us be called sorcerers of your mouthes, we are content, seing our Saviour Christe was saied to have the Divell: but as our Saviour awnswered them *If I by Beelzebub cast out divells, wherby do your children cast them out: but if I by the spirit of God cast out divells, then know that the kingdome of God is come unto you:* even so we awnswer you, if we be sorcerers whie do you call this blessed government as you do in this letter: but if wee by the grace of Gods spirit, have taken in hand this busines of reforming our selves, know you that the sinne of blasphemie which you lay upon other will rest upon your owne skirts. Afterward T. W. using some sharp speach, you tell him his tongue is tipped with a marvailous heate. I never heard of a tongue tipped with heate afore: but I heard that one of your neighbour prechers was sayde to have his tongue tipped with gold & his lippes with silver: but he which spake it might be deceived, for all is not gold that glistereth.

Afterward againe you reckon up a greate sorte of sharpe speaches, which T. W. did use, and you make a bead roule of them: as felow deceivers, false brethren, men pleasers, blinde guides, trees without fruite, etc.: and you say precisely that thei are not wordes proceeding from the Spirit of God: but thei and such like are wordes proceeding from our Saviour Christe, the apostles, and prophetes. therfore by your reason, our Saviour Christe, the apostles, and prophetes had not the spirit of God. I pray you where are these speaches, *generation of vipers, painted sepulchers, hypocrits, foxes, painted walls, adulterous generation, princes of Sodom, people of Gomorrha, trees without fruite, cloudes without rayne,* and a thousand moe[1]. I am sure you know them and where to finde them: so that the most that you could have saide, therfore, had bene that the wrong appliing of these speaches proceeded not from the spirit of God:

[464]
Matt. 12[27]

---

[1] John Field replies in the same way to a similar charge made against Wilcox and himself concerning *An Admonition to the Parliament.* Peel, *Cal. Sec. Parte of a Register,* I. 89.

then if you could have proved them falsie applied, you had
saide something, wheras now being so hastie to give T. W.
a blow, have missed him and striken the childe in his armes,
for you have spoken untruelie of the Spirite of God. but
your proof is because the Spirit of God is gentle : so were
these gentle whome I have named, and Moses was an
exceeding gentle and meeke man, yet was he angrie in the
Lordes quarell in so much that he threw the tables out
his handes, and brake them, he was notablie angrie when
he did that. I know we are to deale with meeknes at the
beginning with them in whome there is hope, & so were
you dealt with, but thei which after two or three admoni-
tions remaine willfull and obstinate, and specially to the
hurt of others are more roughlie to be handled.

   Manie things there are more yea more then as many
more, which for verie want of time and wearines I am faine
to let passe, having in this which I have writen given a
taste of the rest. At last you make a praier, but cleanse
your handes of the bloud of them which perish by your
negligence : for els the prophet Esay telleth you : *though
you make many prayers the Lord will not heare you, your
handes being full of bloud :* as you have prayed in the end
of your letter so do I pray with faithfull Nehemiah, a glasse
for you all if you would looke upon him. I pray I say with [465]
him not in myne owne injurie, but in the Lord his quarell,
not against you if you repent & obey, nor particularlie
against any of your companie, whose repentance I wish
rather, but generallie against the professed enemies which Nehem. 4[4]
will not builde Gods house, and hold backe those that would.
*Heare o our God for we are despised, and turne their shame
upon their owne heades and give them unto a pray in the
land of their captivitie and cover not their iniquitie neyther
let their synne be put out of thy presence, for thei have provoked us before the buylders.*

Not yours excepte you repent

R. H.

INDEX

For EU product safety concerns, contact us at Calle de José Abascal, 56–1°, 28003 Madrid, Spain or eugpsr@cambridge.org.

www.ingramcontent.com/pod-product-compliance
Ingram Content Group UK Ltd.
Pitfield, Milton Keynes, MK11 3LW, UK
UKHW020325140625

459647UK00018B/2009